T0120819

CONTINUING CHRIST'S MISSION

You Too Can Spread God's Word

Robert S. Chambers

WESTBOW
PRESS®
A DIVISION OF THOMAS NELSON
& ZONDERVAN

Copyright © 2022 Robert S. Chambers.

All rights reserved. No part of this book may be used or reproduced by
any means, graphic, electronic, or mechanical, including photocopying,
recording, taping or by any information storage retrieval system
without the written permission of the author except in the case of
brief quotations embodied in critical articles and reviews.

WestBow Press books may be ordered through booksellers or by contacting:

WestBow Press
A Division of Thomas Nelson & Zondervan
1663 Liberty Drive
Bloomington, IN 47403
www.westbowpress.com
844-714-3454

Because of the dynamic nature of the Internet, any web addresses or
links contained in this book may have changed since publication and
may no longer be valid. The views expressed in this work are solely those
of the author and do not necessarily reflect the views of the publisher,
and the publisher hereby disclaims any responsibility for them.

Any people depicted in stock imagery provided by Getty Images are
models, and such images are being used for illustrative purposes only.
Certain stock imagery © Getty Images.

Unless otherwise noted, scripture quotations taken from the (NASB®) New
American Standard Bible®, Copyright © 1960, 1971, 1977, 1995 by The Lockman
Foundation. Used by permission. All rights reserved. www.lockman.org

Additional scripture quotations are from The ESV® Bible (The Holy Bible,
English Standard Version®), copyright © 2001 by Crossway, a publishing
ministry of Good News Publishers. Used by permission. All rights reserved.

Additional scripture taken from the King James Version of the Bible.

ISBN: 978-1-6642-5572-2 (sc)
ISBN: 978-1-6642-5573-9 (hc)
ISBN: 978-1-6642-5571-5 (e)

Library of Congress Control Number: 2022900945

Print information available on the last page.

WestBow Press rev. date: 02/09/2022

To my daughters, Ashley and Ivy, blessings from God.
You have changed my life and made me realize
the awesome responsibility of sharing the gospel.

CONTENTS

Preface

As the apostle Paul was counseling young Timothy, he offered these words of advice.

> Let no one look down on your youthfulness, but rather in speech, conduct, love, faith and purity, show yourself an example of those who believe. Until I come, give attention to the public reading of Scripture, to exhortation and teaching. Do not neglect the spiritual gift within you, which was bestowed on you through prophetic utterance with the laying on of hands by the presbytery. Take pains with these things; be absorbed in them, so that your progress will be evident to all. Pay close attention to yourself and to your teaching; persevere in these things, for as you do this you will ensure salvation both for yourself and for those who hear you. (1 Tim. 4:12–16)

What is it that strikes my heart? It is the steadfast, endless commitment inspired by Paul's exhortation to show yourself an example, give attention to, not neglect, take pains with, be absorbed in, pay close attention to, persevere in—with what result?

"You will ensure salvation both for yourself and for those who hear you."

With these very convictions, I write this book. Whereas my first publication, *A Debt I Cannot Pay*, was a thorough study of the gospel message, this second book, *Continuing Christ's Mission*, is all about preparing Christians to spread that message. The fruit born from what Jesus accomplished is found in the growth of the Body of Christ as new Christians are added to His Church. With the goal of *Continuing Christ's Mission*, I am committed to doing my part to motivate and equip fellow Christians for the task of sharing the good news of Jesus in the twenty-first century.

I addressed these issues previously in a thirteen-week Bible class called Evangelism and the Gospel of Jesus. Three essential elements drove the subject matter.

1. The Message: the gospel, the good news of Jesus, God's plan to save humankind
2. The Messenger: Jesus Christ, the Word, the Son of God
3. The Messaging: evangelism, the act of sharing the good news of Jesus with the world

These are the topics that spawned the writing of this book. In fact, this is essentially the second volume in what could be seen as a two-volume series designed to equip every Christian with the background, knowledge, and resources needed to spread the good news of Jesus.

Taken together, these two books, *A Debt I Cannot Pay* and *Continuing Christ's Mission*, provide individuals and congregations with the instructional content needed to support the work of evangelism. Moreover, these books are ideal for use in classes aimed at recruiting and equipping members to take on a larger role in sharing the gospel with others.

It is my sincere hope and prayer that this book will equip and encourage Christians to make, foster, and grow disciples of Jesus by continuing Christ's mission bringing peace and comfort to struggling souls.

Acknowledgments

I cannot think about evangelism without having the names of George Carman and Tyrone Mynhier pop into my mind. Both are faithful Christian men who have dedicated their lives to spreading the good news of Jesus. By their teaching and example, they have each had a profound impact on my life as a Christian. I am especially indebted to George for reviewing the manuscripts of both books I have published and to Tyrone for his suggestions about how to initiate Bible studies.

I would also like to acknowledge my wife, Janet, who helped me edit and proofread the text of this book, and my daughters and sons-in-law, Ashley and Keith Guerra and Ivy and Ruben Baca, for serving as sounding boards for ideas involving the work in progress.

Finally, my sincere thanks go to Ruben for all the expertise, creative development, and support he has provided for my website at www.TheTruthTransforms.com.

1

Of Men or of God?

AFTER FIGHTING THIS MOVEMENT FOR THREE YEARS, THE religious establishment had orchestrated the death of the ringleader, and now life would finally get back to normal—or would it? Such was the hope of the Jewish council, but that was not to be. When the apostles refused to stop teaching, the Jewish leaders were prepared to put them to death until one of their own, Gamaliel, offered stark words of warning:

> And he said to them, "Men of Israel, take care what
> you propose to do with these men. For some time
> ago Theudas rose up, claiming to be somebody,
> and a group of about four hundred men joined up
> with him. But he was killed, and all who followed
> him were dispersed and came to nothing. After
> this man, Judas of Galilee rose up in the days
> of the census and drew away some people after

him; he too perished, and all those who followed him were scattered. So in the present case, I say to you, stay away from these men and let them alone, for if this plan or action is of men, it will be overthrown; but if it is of God, you will not be able to overthrow them; or else you may even be found fighting against God." They took his advice; and after calling the apostles in, they flogged them and ordered them not to speak in the name of Jesus, and then released them. (Acts 5:35–40)

The rest is history. Christianity spread throughout the world as faithful disciples devoted themselves to continuing Christ's mission according to God's plan.

But if Gamaliel were alive today, might he see things differently? Would he witness an apathy among church members content to warm the pews in weekly services, and conclude that perhaps Christianity is simply an action of humankind destined to fade with time? What has changed? The need for the gospel has never been greater, and yet recruiting members to engage in evangelism seems to get harder and harder.

To many, evangelism is the job of the pastors and deacons, and indeed it is. However, it does not stop with them. Church leaders are not member proxies, nor were they ever intended to be. The church is made up of many members, and its growth depends on the contributions of each individual in the body (Eph. 4:14–16).

Although every Christian is to have a role in continuing Christ's mission, some struggle to find it, and others are content to sit on the sidelines. If the church is to be the salt of the earth and the light of the world as Jesus intended (Matt. 5:13–16), then that must change. Therein lies the purpose for this book: to motivate and equip Christians for the task of continuing Christ's mission by

- defining the mission and message,
- addressing the obstacles and fears that limit participation,
- identifying roles for member involvement,
- equipping Christians for evangelistic service, and
- introducing tools for evangelism through the website www.TheTruthTransforms.com.

CHAPTER

Jesus: the Messenger and His Message

J ESUS WAS GOD'S ULTIMATE MESSENGER TO THE WORLD.

> God, after He spoke long ago to the fathers in the prophets in many portions and in many ways, in these last days has spoken to us in His Son, whom He appointed heir of all things, through whom also He made the world. And He is the radiance of His glory and the exact representation of His nature, and upholds all things by the word of His power. When He had made purification of sins, He sat down at the right hand of the Majesty on high. (Heb. 1:1–3)

Within this passage, the preeminence of Jesus is clearly seen. He is the Son of God, heir of all things, Creator who upholds all things, and now is seated at the right hand of the Majesty on high. Equally impressive is what Jesus was able to accomplish during His brief time on earth. He spoke on behalf of God (revelation), exemplified the nature of the Heavenly Father (modeled holiness), and purified sins (sanctification/redemption). No other person has had such an impact on the course of human history.

The ministry of Jesus was initiated under the direction of the Heavenly Father. In the words of Jesus, "I can do nothing on My own initiative. As I hear, I judge; and My judgment is just, because I do not seek My own will, but the will of Him who sent Me" (John 5:30).

As God's messenger, Jesus amazed the crowds with His teaching, for He spoke as one having authority in a manner quite different from their scribes (Matt. 7:28–29). His message came directly from God, the Father:

> Do you not believe that I am in the Father, and the Father is in Me? The words that I say to you I do not speak on My own initiative, but the Father abiding in Me does His works. (John 14:10)

> He who does not love Me does not keep My words; and the word which you hear is not Mine, but the Father's who sent Me. (John 14:24)

Although Jesus had great compassion for people and sought to comfort them and alleviate their physical suffering, His priority was revealing divine truth. That message was spiritual in nature and focused on the kingdom of God:

> When day came, Jesus left and went to a secluded place; and the crowds were searching for Him, and

> came to Him and tried to keep Him from going away from them. But He said to them, "I must preach the kingdom of God to the other cities also, for I was sent for this purpose." (Luke 4:42–43)

Within the message that Jesus delivered to humankind were the words of life—words pointing to the futility of the flesh (John 6:63) and offering a more important prospect of eternal life (John 6:68) enabled by nurturing an inner spirit that will endure beyond the grave.

The importance of God's message is evident by the fact that He sent His Son to proclaim it. Jesus warned about the judgment facing those who reject Him and what He had to say: "He who rejects Me and does not receive My sayings, has one who judges him; the word I spoke is what will judge him at the last day" (John 12:48).

The first-century believers embraced God's message with thanksgiving and joy, and it changed their lives.

> So then, those who had received his word were baptized; and that day there were added about three thousand souls. They were continually devoting themselves to the apostles' teaching and to fellowship, to the breaking of bread and to prayer. (Acts 2:41–42)

So committed were these Christians that even after the stoning of Stephen, when persecution arose against the early church, they carried the message of Jesus with them as they were scattered abroad.

And on that day a great persecution began against the church in Jerusalem, and they were all scattered throughout the regions of Judea and Samaria, except the apostles. Some devout men buried Stephen, and made loud lamentation over him. But Saul began ravaging the church, entering house after house, and dragging off men and women, he would put them in prison. Therefore, those who had been scattered went about preaching the word. (Acts 8:1–4)

As disciples of Jesus, these faithful followers became God's early messengers, continuing Christ's mission and establishing the pattern for church growth. Christians living today are also God's messengers, charged with teaching the saving message of Jesus throughout the whole world. Every time we leave home, we are entering the mission field.

CHAPTER

Jesus: His Mission

JESUS CAME TO EARTH ON A "MISSION," A WORD DERIVED FROM a Latin word meaning "to send." He was dispatched by God for an assigned purpose, a fact attested to by Jesus in John 6:38: "For I have come down from heaven, not to do My own will, but the will of Him who sent Me."

What was God's will? Jesus answered that in Luke, chapter 19, during His encounter with Zacchaeus, a rich tax collector. So anxious was Zacchaeus to see Jesus that he ran ahead and climbed a tree, waiting for Jesus to pass by. Much to his surprise, Jesus not only acknowledged Zacchaeus but chose to stay with him, an encounter that led Zacchaeus to donate half his wealth to the poor and to pay fourfold restitution to any he had defrauded. On witnessing this, Jesus said, "Today salvation has come to this house, because he, too, is a son of Abraham. For the Son of Man has come to seek and to save that which was lost" (Luke 19:9–10).

Jesus claimed that His mission was to the lost and that it had two distinct parts, *seeking* and *saving*. More often than not, when Luke 19:10 is read, the emphasis is placed on the saving part, and seeking gets glossed over. Unfortunately, to do so overlooks the significance of the entirety of what actually takes place in the process of evangelism. One first must seek out and connect with the lost in order to have an opportunity to save them. Jesus recognized this fact, and that is why He spent so much of His time among the scorned of society. His doing so grieved many religious leaders of the day, who complained about Jesus and His disciples and believed their own commitment to holiness should have precluded them from associating with sinners. Jesus addressed those concerns by reminding them of the true mission:

> And Levi gave a big reception for Him in his house; and there was a great crowd of tax collectors and other people who were reclining at the table with them. The Pharisees and their scribes began grumbling at His disciples, saying, "Why do you eat and drink with the tax collectors and sinners?" And Jesus answered and said to them, "It is not those who are well who need a physician, but those who are sick. I have not come to call the righteous but sinners to repentance." (Luke 5:29–32)

Jesus was seeking and saving the lost by calling sinners to repent.

There is a powerful lesson in what took place at Levi's reception, and it involves making the proper distinction between sin and the sinner. As the Creator, God expects us to be obedient children conforming to His holy nature (1 Pet. 1:14–16). However, even though sin spiritually separates humankind from a holy God (Isa. 59:1–2), it does not undermine God's love for sinners. Being created in the image of God (Gen. 1:26–27) makes human beings unique, possessing an eternal spirit in the likeness of God as Spirit. That spiritual bond explains the great lengths to which God was willing to go to restore and preserve His relationship with humankind.

> For God so loved the world, that He gave His only begotten Son, that whoever believes in Him shall not perish, but have eternal life. For God did not send the Son into the world to judge the world, but that the world might be saved through Him. (John 3:16–17)

Jesus did not go to the cross to save the righteous. On the contrary, Paul said: "For while we were still helpless, at the right time Christ died for the ungodly" (Rom. 5:6). Jesus died for sinners (Rom. 5:8). That is the reason Jesus spent so much of His ministry reaching out to the lost (i.e., *seeking* them). Luke dedicated an entire chapter to the parables Jesus taught on this subject: the lost sheep (Luke 15:3–6), the lost coin (Luke 15:8–10), and the well-known parable of the prodigal son (Luke 15:11–32). In each case, Jesus emphasized the commitment and joy of finding and restoring the lost.

To make His priority and focus even clearer, Jesus said: "I tell you that in the same way, there will be more joy in heaven over one sinner who repents than over ninety–nine righteous persons who need no repentance" (Luke 15:7). Where do today's Christians find joy and commitment? Do we spend more time and effort seeking the lost or glorifying the righteous? What would Jesus say?

While seeking the lost is important, it is not enough for Christians simply to spend time with sinners, hoping something good will rub off on them. When Jesus began His ministry, He admonished sinners, calling them to repent while informing them that the Kingdom of Heaven is at hand (Matt. 4:17). He delivered a spiritual warning and message that needed to be heard—the truth about judgment, repentance, and reconciliation through words that can free sinners from the burdens of sin.

> So Jesus was saying to those Jews who had believed Him, "If you continue in My word, then you are truly disciples of Mine; and you will know the truth, and the truth will make you free." (John 8:31–32)

God wants all humankind to be saved (1 Tim. 2:3–4) and sent His Son as the messenger of truth to seek and save the lost. Since "all have sinned and fall short of the glory of God" (Rom. 3:23), all need to hear the good news of Jesus. Only through Him can we obtain the forgiveness of sins and be reconciled to God (Acts 4:12, John 14:6).

Zacchaeus is an excellent example of how Jesus changes the life of those who believe in Him and obey His will. God's plan to save humankind began with Jesus, but it did not end there. Christ's mission continues through the work of His people.

CHAPTER

Christian Works

WHAT ARE CHRISTIAN WORKS? THESE ARE CERTAINLY NOT things done to earn salvation. Rather, they are behaviors or actions embraced as part of a Christian's faith and service. Make no mistake: good works can never blot out sins. A lawbreaker who does good deeds is still guilty of having broken the law. If sinners could save themselves by earning their salvation through works, then that would mean Jesus died on the cross needlessly. Such is not the case.

Paul set the record straight in Ephesians 2:8: "For by grace you have been saved through faith; and that not of yourselves, it is the gift of God." The source of our salvation stems solely from the gift of a loving God and the grace He bestows on faithful, obedient believers through the sacrifice of His Holy Son.

> He Himself bore our sins in His body on the
> cross, so that we might die to sin and live to

righteousness; for by His wounds you were healed. (1 Pet. 2:24)

And having been made perfect, He became to all those who obey Him the source of eternal salvation. (Heb. 5:9)

Paul explained that salvation is "not as a result of works, so that no one may boast" (Eph. 2:9). Salvation by works would promote human inequality by setting people apart and giving individuals something to brag about. A perfect example is found in the account of the Pharisee and the tax collector, who both went to the temple to pray.

The Pharisee stood and was praying this to himself: "God, I thank You that I am not like other people: swindlers, unjust, adulterers, or even like this tax collector. I fast twice a week; I pay tithes of all that I get." But the tax collector, standing some distance away, was even unwilling to lift up his eyes to heaven, but was beating his breast, saying, "God, be merciful to me, the sinner!" I tell you, this man went to his house justified rather than the other; for everyone who exalts himself will be humbled, but he who humbles himself will be exalted. (Luke 18:11–14)

The Pharisee exalted himself believing that his good works (fasting and tithing) made him better than the tax collector. He failed to acknowledge that he too was a sinner. Judging individuals based on how much good they have done creates a false sense of worth. It denies the fact that God is impartial (Rom. 2:11) and that He values all humans equally because all possess an eternal spirit, having been created in the image of God (Gen. 1:26–27).

In Matthew 23, Jesus criticized the scribes and Pharisees for setting themselves apart by seeking special recognition and places of honor. His reasoning was easy to understand: God alone reigns supreme, and all others serve Him as equal brethren.

> But do not be called Rabbi; for One is your Teacher, and you are all brothers. Do not call anyone on earth your father; for One is your Father, He who is in heaven. (Matt. 23:8–9)

Since good works don't earn salvation, then why do them? Christians do good works because that is what God expects them to do. It was God's intent from the beginning. "For we are His workmanship, created in Christ Jesus for good works, which God prepared beforehand so that we would walk in them" (Eph. 2:10). God's influence in the world today can be seen in the actions of His people loving others as we love ourselves (Matt. 22:39).

Through the grace afforded in the sacrifice of Jesus on the cross, a sinner can become a new creature (2 Cor. 5:17), holy and righteous, continuing the work of Jesus as God's representative on earth: "for it is God who is at work in you, both to will and to work for His good pleasure" (Phil. 2:13). This is how Christians add light to a dark world and bring glory to God (Matt. 5:14–16).

Doing good is a Christian's duty. Jesus said it is merely doing what ought to be done in accordance with God's will: "So you too, when you do all the things which are commanded you, say, 'We are unworthy slaves; we have done only that which we ought to have done'" (Luke 17:10). Christians should not look to earn any special consideration for doing the right thing. God expects such behavior even if it is painful. "For what credit is there if, when you sin and are harshly treated, you endure it with patience? But if when you do what is right and suffer for it you patiently endure it, this finds favor with God" (1 Pet. 2:20).

Christians are drawn to do good works not because they have to but because they want to. It comes naturally for those who love the Lord and seek to please Him. Jesus said, "If you love Me, you will keep My commandments" (John 14:15). As disciples of Jesus, Christians follow His lead in striving to be holy as God is holy and doing just what He would do.

> As obedient children, do not be conformed to the former lusts which were yours in your ignorance, but like the Holy One who called you, be holy yourselves also in all your behavior; because it is written, "You shall be holy, for I am holy." (1 Pet. 1:14–16)

Works arise naturally from a Christian's faith in God. Works and faith go hand in hand. Without them, that faith is dead and worthless: "For just as the body without the spirit is dead, so also faith without works is dead" (Jas. 2:26).

Christians undergo a marvelous transformation during their spiritual rebirth.

> Or do you not know that all of us who have been baptized into Christ Jesus have been baptized into His death? Therefore we have been buried with Him through baptism into death, so that as Christ was raised from the dead through the glory of the

> Father, so we too might walk in newness of life. For if we have become united with Him in the likeness of His death, certainly we shall also be in the likeness of His resurrection, knowing this, that our old self was crucified with Him, in order that our body of sin might be done away with, so that we would no longer be slaves to sin; for he who has died is freed from sin. (Rom. 6:3–7)

Paul explained the identity change that comes from being baptized. The old sinful self is crucified, put to death in the waters of baptism, shedding the body of sin to walk in newness of life, having been forgiven and cleansed by the blood of Christ.

In this life-changing moment, Christians give their lives to Jesus and become vessels of God on earth, with Christ living in and working through them. This allows the good works that Jesus initiated to continue in His absence on earth through the workings of His people (i.e., Christians).

> I have been crucified with Christ; and it is no longer I who live, but Christ lives in me; and the life which I now live in the flesh I live by faith in the Son of God, who loved me and gave Himself up for me. (Gal. 2:20).

In Ephesians 4:11–12, Paul discussed God's efforts to equip Christians for those works of service. God provided inspired instructors to build up the Body of Christ "until we all attain to the unity of the faith, and of the knowledge of the Son of God, to a mature man, to the measure of the stature which belongs to the fullness of Christ" (Eph. 4:13). Maturing to become spiritually

Christlike is necessary to achieve the ultimate goal: the stability and growth of the Church.

> As a result, we are no longer to be children, tossed here and there by waves and carried about by every wind of doctrine, by the trickery of men, by craftiness in deceitful scheming; but speaking the truth in love, we are to grow up in all aspects into Him who is the head, even Christ, from whom the whole body, being fitted and held together by what every joint supplies, according to the proper working of each individual part, causes the growth of the body for the building up of itself in love. (Eph. 4:14–16)

The unity and growth of the Lord's Church depends on the proper working and contributions of each and every member. These good works provide a solid foundation from which to continue Christ's mission of seeking and saving the lost.

CHAPTER

The Christian Mission

Aʟʟ ᴛᴏᴏ ᴏꜰᴛᴇɴ, ᴄʜᴜʀᴄʜɢᴏᴇʀs ᴍᴀᴋᴇ ᴛʜᴇ ᴍɪsᴛᴀᴋᴇ ᴏꜰ thinking a long list of good works somehow fulfills their Christian mission, not realizing what their God–given mission actually is. While it is true that Christians are to lead a good moral life and perform a variety of good deeds in a demonstration of faith stemming from their change in heart, that alone is not the primary mission God has set forth.

The Christian's true mission is what Paul called the ministry of reconciliation.

> Therefore if anyone is in Christ, he is a new creature; the old things passed away; behold, new things have come. Now all these things are from God, who reconciled us to Himself through Christ and gave us the ministry of reconciliation, namely, that God was in Christ reconciling the world to

Himself, not counting their trespasses against them, and He has committed to us the word of reconciliation. Therefore, we are ambassadors for Christ, as though God were making an appeal through us; we beg you on behalf of Christ, be reconciled to God. (2 Cor. 5:17–20)

These four verses are packed full of instruction and insight into God's plans for the Church. First, note that Paul is speaking about anyone in Christ. Who are these people, and how did they get into Christ? They are Christians—those who have been baptized into Christ: "For you are all sons of God through faith in Christ Jesus. For all of you who were baptized into Christ have clothed yourselves with Christ" (Gal. 3:26–27).

Christians are rejuvenated sinners, made new by what God has done in reconciling them through His Son, not counting their trespasses against them. Along with the blessing of forgiveness comes commitment. God committed to Christians the word of reconciliation, the saving message of Jesus that is to be shared with those who are lost.

To define the role Christians are to play in fulfilling their newfound mission, Paul provided a vivid description: "We are ambassadors for Christ, as though God were making an appeal through us; we beg you on behalf of Christ, be reconciled to God" (2 Cor. 5:20). This choice of words is no accident. An ambassador is an accredited diplomat who is an official representative of a body. In this case, the body is the Body of Christ, His Church, and the supreme authority of that body is Jesus.

Christians are ambassadors who represent Jesus. To make this even clearer, Paul goes on to define the actual duty of the ambassadors. They are to speak as though Christ were making an appeal directly through them, begging the lost to be reconciled to God. Therein is the true mission that God has assigned to all Christians.

Our mission as Christians entails what Christ declared for Himself in Luke 19:10. It is the same mission that Jesus assigned to the apostles in the Great Commission (Matt. 28:19–20). We are to seek and to save the lost.

Feeding the poor, visiting the sick, caring for the needy, supporting widows and orphans, and loving and projecting kindness in words and deeds are all good works Christians should do. They demonstrate a godly compassion for humankind and make the world a better place. However, without tending to the spiritual needs of the lost, all these physical blessings are done in vain. Jesus summed it up best in Matthew 16:26: "For what will it profit a man if he gains the whole world and forfeits his soul? Or what will a man give in exchange for his soul?"

The Christian's mission is to save souls.

CHAPTER

Evangelism

Evangelism is soul saving. It is publicly and privately preaching and teaching the gospel message to further God's kingdom by making, fostering, and growing disciples of Jesus Christ. Evangelism is the core mission delegated to each and every Christian.

In John 4, Jesus had a life-changing encounter with a Samaritan woman at Jacob's well. After learning that this prophet was actually the Messiah, she returned to the city, proclaiming the news and drawing people to come and see for themselves. As Jesus gathered His disciples and looked up at the oncoming crowds, He said, "Do you not say, 'There are yet four months, and then comes the harvest'? Behold, I say to you, lift up your eyes and look on the fields, that they are white for harvest" (John 4:35). Jesus recognized the opportunity before Him to save souls in a harvest that was ripe for the taking.

The gospel is for everyone (Rom. 1:16). God "desires all men to be saved and to come to the knowledge of the truth" (1 Tim. 2:4). However, for that to happen, Christians must be willing to share the saving message of Jesus. Out of His love for humanity, God has withheld judgment, allowing more time for Christians to seek and save the lost by bringing them to repentance (2 Pet. 3:7–9).

During His time on earth, "Jesus was going through all the cities and villages, teaching in their synagogues and proclaiming the gospel of the kingdom, and healing every kind of disease and every kind of sickness. Seeing the people, He felt compassion for them, because they were distressed and dispirited like sheep without a shepherd" (Matt. 9:35–36). Jesus saw people who were physically hurting, and having compassion for them, He tended to their physical needs, but that was not His sole concern.

Jesus saw an even greater necessity for people who were spiritually struggling and lost. They were disheartened, lacking the hope, peace, and comfort that a loving God could provide. "Then He said to His disciples, 'The harvest is plentiful, but the workers are few. Therefore beseech the Lord of the harvest to send out workers into His harvest'" (Matt. 9:37–38). Jesus recognized that in order to tend to the souls of this crop, more helpers would be needed. What was true two thousand years ago is still true today. God calls on all Christians to take up their mission and go into the harvest as His workers.

There is urgency in the appeal for harvest workers. Evangelism is a priority of the Church. Sin is real. It touches all our lives and with it brings spiritual death breaking the bonds of fellowship with a holy and just God. A Day of Judgment is coming.

> Therefore having overlooked the times of ignorance, God is now declaring to men that all people everywhere should repent, because He

has fixed a day in which He will judge the world
in righteousness through a Man whom He has
appointed, having furnished proof to all men by
raising Him from the dead. (Acts 17:30–31)

Sinners, those who do not know God and those who do not
obey the gospel of Jesus Christ and avail themselves of His saving
grace and mercy, are at risk of eternal separation from God in
Hell (2 Thess. 1:7–9). Harvest workers are needed to lead them to
Jesus, the only way out (Acts 4:12). What could possibly be more
important than saving lost souls?

The reality is many people are lost, separated spiritually from
God by their sin, and don't know it, either because they have
never heard the truth or because they have been deceived by false
teachings. The disastrous outcome is the same—an eternity apart
from God in Hell.

Enter through the narrow gate; for the gate is wide
and the way is broad that leads to destruction, and
there are many who enter through it. For the gate
is small and the way is narrow that leads to life,
and there are few who find it. (Matt. 7:13–14)

Beware of the false prophets, who come to you
in sheep's clothing, but inwardly are ravenous
wolves. (Matt. 7:15)

Not everyone who says to Me, 'Lord, Lord,' will
enter the kingdom of heaven, but he who does
the will of My Father who is in heaven will enter.
Many will say to Me on that day, 'Lord, Lord,

did we not prophesy in Your name, and in Your name cast out demons, and in Your name perform many miracles?' And then I will declare to them, 'I never knew you; depart from Me, you who practice lawlessness'. (Matt. 7:21–23)

How can intellectually honest believers fail to take up the mission and challenge of sharing the gospel message with those who so desperately need to hear it?

CHAPTER

Fulfilling the Christian Mission

THE CHRISTIAN'S MISSION IS WELL DEFINED: TO CONTINUE Christ's mission by seeking and saving the lost. But how is that done? The apostle Paul actually summarized the key steps involved in evangelism.

> For there is no distinction between Jew and Greek; for the same Lord is Lord of all, abounding in riches for all who call on Him; for "Whoever will call on the name of the Lord will be saved." How then will they call on Him in whom they have not believed? How will they believe in Him whom they have not heard? And how will they hear without a preacher? How will they preach unless they are sent? Just as it is written, "How beautiful are the

feet of those who bring good news of good things!"
(Rom. 10:12–15)

Paul defines the conversion process in reverse order, starting from the desired outcome and working back to the beginning.

Whoever will call on the name of the Lord will be saved.

Here Paul identifies the end goal and how it is attained. People are *saved* by making an appeal directly to God. He alone is the source of salvation, and it is not earned. It is a gift offered to all humanity by the grace and mercy of a loving Heavenly Father. Although the religious world professes many different beliefs and explanations for how individuals call on the name of the Lord to be saved, God's directive is the only one that matters.

The best commentary on scripture comes from other scriptures. Peter resolved the matter in 1 Peter 3:21, "Corresponding to that, baptism now saves you—not the removal of dirt from the flesh, but an appeal to God for a good conscience—through the resurrection of Jesus Christ." It is during the act of baptism that sinners call on the name of the Lord, making an appeal to God for a good conscience (i.e., cleansing of sin). The power of forgiveness does not come from the physical act of washing but through the resurrection of Jesus.

Saul's conversion account confirms that baptism is the way sinners call on the name of the Lord. After spending three days in prayer and fasting, a repentant Saul received instructions from Ananias on what he still must do to obtain the forgiveness of his sins: "Now why do you delay? Get up and be baptized, and wash away your sins, calling on His name" (Acts 22:16). Note two very significant points. First, even after spending three days in prayer and fasting, Saul's sins were not yet forgiven. Second, Ananias told Saul how to wash away his sins by calling on the name of the Lord. It was by being baptized in the name of Jesus, just as was written in 1 Peter 3:21 and was done on the day of Pentecost.

> Now when they heard this, they were pierced to the heart, and said to Peter and the rest of the apostles, "Brethren, what shall we do?" Peter said to them, "Repent, and each of you be baptized in the name of Jesus Christ for the forgiveness of your sins; and you will receive the gift of the Holy Spirit" (Acts 2:37–38)

> So then, those who had received his word were baptized; and that day there were added about three thousand souls. (Acts 2:41)

> And the Lord was adding to their number day by day those who were being saved. (Acts 2:47)

Salvation is bestowed on faithful, obedient believers who call on the name of the Lord by being baptized in the name of Jesus. Jesus then adds these saved to His Church.

How then will they call on Him in whom they have not believed?

The Bible makes it clear that *belief* in Jesus is absolutely necessary for salvation.

> Therefore I said to you that you will die in your sins; for unless you believe that I am He, you will die in your sins. (John 8:24)

He who has believed and has been baptized shall
be saved; but he who has disbelieved shall be
condemned. (Mark 16:16)

God does not force Himself on anyone. He seeks willing and informed followers. Before calling on the name of the Lord, sinners must be convinced about the true identity of Jesus as the Son of God and their need for the salvation He offers to humankind. They must be made aware of their alienation from God, the danger that entails, and the forgiveness that is available through the sacrifice of Jesus. Minds must be changed and hearts converted, leading to repentance.

How will they believe in Him whom they have not heard?

To embrace the truth, one must first *hear* it. That is the message of Jesus. It is the gospel, "the power of God for salvation to everyone who believes" (Rom. 1:16). Hearts are convicted by understanding the things God has revealed. Jesus said that is the role of the Holy Spirit, convicting the world concerning sin (John 16:8).

A Christian's faith is not a blind faith. "Faith comes from hearing, and hearing by the word of Christ" (Rom. 10:17). We contact the words of Christ today through the inspired text of the New Testament. In the words of Jesus, "He who has ears, let him hear" (Matt. 13:9).

There is logic behind God's plan to save humankind. Isaiah pointed to that fact in his prophesy from God to the nation of Israel: "'Come now, and let us reason together,' Says the LORD, 'Though your sins are as scarlet, They will be as white as snow; Though they are red like crimson, They will be like wool'" (Isa. 1:18). God appeals to our sense of reason, but people must hear and comprehend His message in order to believe.

And how will they hear without a preacher?

The message of Jesus is spread by Christians willing to *preach*. Someone must take on the task of leading people to the truth, as is illustrated in Acts 8, where an angel of the Lord directed Philip to the Ethiopian eunuch for that very purpose.

> Philip ran up and heard him reading Isaiah the prophet, and said, "Do you understand what you are reading?" And he said, "Well, how could I, unless someone guides me?" And he invited Philip to come up and sit with him. (Acts 8:30–31)

> Then Philip opened his mouth, and beginning from this Scripture he preached Jesus to him. (Acts 8:35)

Many have never heard the message of Jesus in its pure state. They are ignorant of their predicament and the dangers confronting them. Others have a false sense of security, believing all is well when in fact they have been misled by false teachers and human doctrines. Unless these individuals are enlightened by the biblical truth, they are doomed for eternity. Hence the genuine need for "harvest workers"—Christians who are willing to seek out and carry the truth to the lost.

How will they preach unless they are sent?

The authority for evangelism comes directly from God and is well established by the directives He issued to and through the apostles. God *sent* His followers on a mission.

> Go therefore and make disciples of all the nations, baptizing them in the name of the Father and the Son and the Holy Spirit, teaching them to observe all that I commanded you; and lo, I am with you always, even to the end of the age. (Matt. 28:19–20)

> Therefore, we are ambassadors for Christ, as though God were making an appeal through us; we beg you on behalf of Christ, be reconciled to God. (2 Cor. 5:20)

> But sanctify Christ as Lord in your hearts, always being ready to make a defense to everyone who asks you to give an account for the hope that is in you, yet with gentleness and reverence. (1 Pet. 3:15)

Jesus never intended for Christians to conceal their faith. That is why He called for His disciples to be the salt of the earth and the light of the world (Matt. 5:13–16).

Evangelism is driven by the passion, vision, and commitment to save lost souls. Many of the Lord's harvest workers come directly from excited new converts who have been mentored to share the blessings they have received in Christ. Others arise as missionaries dispatched by local congregations into the fields white for harvest. But truth be told, we all have been *sent* to engage in the Lord's work of seeking and saving the lost.

CHAPTER

The Obstacles

WHY IS THERE SUCH A SHORTAGE OF "HARVEST WORKERS"?
Even Jesus encountered this problem during his ministry on earth,
so much so that He encouraged followers to fervently call for the
Lord to send out more workers into the harvest (Matt. 9:37–38).

If souls are to be saved, then Christians must be actively seeking
and teaching the lost. God commanded it, and the message is well
defined, so why are most Christians so reluctant to get involved
in evangelism?

To answer that question, it is useful to examine God's calling to
Moses. Moses is known as a man of great faith, and his relationship
to God was truly unique. "Thus the LORD used to speak to Moses
face to face, just as a man speaks to his friend" (Exod. 33:11).
However, even this prophet had a rough start.

As Moses was tending the sheep of his father-in-law Jethro, an
angel of the Lord appeared to him in a blazing fire from the midst
of a burning bush. From that bush came the voice of the Lord.

> The Lord said, "I have surely seen the affliction of My people who are in Egypt, and have given heed to their cry because of their taskmasters, for I am aware of their sufferings." (Exod. 3:7)

> "Therefore, come now, and I will send you to Pharaoh, so that you may bring My people, the sons of Israel, out of Egypt." (Exod. 3:10)

Moses was given a mission. God commanded him to approach Pharaoh as God's delegated messenger in order to free Israel and bring the people out of Egypt. Notice how Moses responded to God's calling:

> But Moses said to God, "Who am I, that I should go to Pharaoh, and that I should bring the sons of Israel out of Egypt?" (Exod. 3:11)

Moses immediately began questioning his suitability and qualifications for the job. In all likelihood, he was thinking to himself, "Why me, Lord?" Perhaps fostering low self-esteem and most certainly lacking in confidence, Moses was looking for a way out. Surely there was someone better equipped for this mission. Notice how the Lord responded to Moses. God said, "Certainly I will be with you" (Exod. 3:12). Moses was not being abandoned and sent on this fearful mission alone. God was going to be by his side every step of the way.

As he pondered the task before him, Moses worried what could happen, fearing mission failure or outright rejection by the Israelites. He began to wonder how he could possibly deal with all the difficult situations that might arise. "What if" scenarios bounced around in his head.

> Then Moses said to God, "Behold, I am going to
> the sons of Israel, and I will say to them, 'The God
> of your fathers has sent me to you.' Now they may
> say to me, 'What is His name?' What shall I say to
> them?" (Exod. 3:13)

His first quandary was how to convince the Israelites that indeed the God of their fathers had sent him on this mission. Moses imagined the need for a name, the identity of the sender.

> God said to Moses, "I AM WHO I AM"; and He said,
> "Thus you shall say to the sons of Israel, 'I AM has
> sent me to you.'" (Exod. 3:14).

God exists! These words ("I AM") are the hallmark of the living God—words carried over into the New Testament by Jesus Himself as He proclaimed His deity (John 8:58). What followed in Exodus 3:15–22 were God's instructions to Moses, revealing the specific things he was to say and do as well as a description of what the outcome of His mission would be.

Moving on from that question, Moses posed yet another.

> Then Moses said, "What if they will not believe
> me or listen to what I say? For they may say, 'The
> LORD has not appeared to you.'" (Exod. 4:1).

In response, God promised Moses supernatural abilities that could only come through miracles empowered by the Creator of the universe. He would be able to turn his staff into a snake, afflict and heal his hand with leprosy, and change water from the Nile River into blood (Exod. 4:2–9). Here again, God patiently calmed the fears of Moses.

Unable to dissuade God with these what-ifs, Moses then focused on his self-perceived inadequacies of speech.

> Then Moses said to the LORD, "Please, Lord, I have never been eloquent, neither recently nor in time past, nor since You have spoken to Your servant; for I am slow of speech and slow of tongue." (Exod. 4:10)

Despite the concerns of Moses, God was having none of that, and His retort was clear.

> The LORD said to him, "Who has made man's mouth? Or who makes him mute or deaf, or seeing or blind? Is it not I, the LORD? Now then go, and I, even I, will be with your mouth, and teach you what you are to say." (Exod. 4:11–12)

In these words, God was reminding Moses of what He had told him earlier. Moses was not undertaking this mission by his own power and abilities. God was going to be with him, equipping him for success (Exod. 3:12). It would be God speaking through him to execute the mission at hand.

Despite God's encouragement, Moses remained unconvinced and expressed his lack of faith, saying: "Please, Lord, now send the message by whomever You will" (Exod. 4:13). The English Standard Version (ESV) translates this verse with a clearer meaning: "Oh, my Lord, please send someone else." Moses wanted to pass the burden and responsibility from himself to some other person. Proof that Moses was in fact asking God to unburden him from this mission can be seen in God's reaction.

> Then the anger of the LORD burned against
> Moses, and He said, "Is there not your brother
> Aaron the Levite? I know that he speaks fluently.
> And moreover, behold, he is coming out to meet
> you; when he sees you, he will be glad in his heart.
> You are to speak to him and put the words in his
> mouth; and I, even I, will be with your mouth and
> his mouth, and I will teach you what you are to do.
> Moreover, he shall speak for you to the people; and
> he will be as a mouth for you and you will be as
> God to him." (Exod. 4:14–16)

God was not pleased with Moses. However, despite His anger, God accommodated Moses, allowing him to speak God's words to the nation of Israel through the mouth of his brother Aaron.

What can be learned from the experience of Moses? Consider how he reacted to God's calling by

- questioning his qualifications and suitability for the mission based on his low self-esteem and lack of confidence
- worrying about what-ifs—the things that might befall him
- fearing failure and rejection
- pleading inadequacy of speech, not knowing what to say and believing himself not to be a polished speaker

Moses artificially erected many obstacles in his mind. He had no trouble coming up with excuses and reasons why he was not the right person for the job. And yet—God chose Moses, and God does not make mistakes!

CHAPTER

The Challenge

JUST AS MOSES WAS CHOSEN BY GOD FOR THE MISSION OF freeing Israel from Egyptian bondage, so too Christians today have been chosen by God to free fellow humans from the bondage of sin.

> But you are a chosen race, a royal priesthood, a holy nation, a people for God's own possession, so that you may proclaim the excellencies of Him who has called you out of darkness into His marvelous light. (1 Pet. 2:9)

God has given us the "ministry of reconciliation" and appointed us to be "ambassadors for Christ" to the world "as though God were making an appeal through us," begging humanity to be reconciled to God through His Son (2 Cor. 5:18–20).

How do most Christians react when confronted with this mission assignment? The typical reaction involves

- questioning our qualifications and suitability for the mission based on low self-esteem and lack of confidence
- worrying about what-ifs—the things that might befall us
- fearing failure and rejection
- pleading inadequacy of speech—not knowing what to say and not being a polished speaker

We tend to react in the same way Moses reacted ... and yet, God has chosen us too! And God does not make mistakes.

The devil is real. He wants us to fail, and he promotes our misgivings: "Be of sober spirit, be on the alert. Your adversary, the devil, prowls around like a roaring lion, seeking someone to devour" (1 Pet. 5:8). We must not give in to anxieties and fears but must remain strong and resist the pleas of the devil.

So what is the lesson for Christians today? Even though we may not feel up to the task that God has assigned to us, God knows best. Just as God accompanied Moses on his mission, so too will He be with His ambassadors for Christ. The promise that God made to be with Moses on his mission (Exod. 3:12) was likewise given during the Great Commission to those Jesus sent to seek and save the lost: "and lo, I am with you always, even to the end of the age" (Matt. 28:20).

Paul too acknowledged the presence and power of Jesus as he took up Christ's mission following his fateful encounter with the Lord on the road to Damascus.

> I have been crucified with Christ; and it is no longer I who live, but Christ lives in me; and the life which I now live in the flesh I live by faith in the Son of God, who loved me and gave Himself up for me. (Gal. 2:20)

> We proclaim Him, admonishing every man and teaching every man with all wisdom, so that we may present every man complete in Christ. For this purpose also I labor, striving according to His power, which mightily works within me. (Col. 1:28–29)

Very often Christians become discouraged thinking evangelism is something they must do by themselves without the help of other brothers and sisters in Christ. While it is true that some like to go forth seeking and saving the lost carrying only a Bible in hand and God in heart, that is not well suited to everyone. Indeed, Jesus saw value in sending forth His disciples in pairs: "Now after this the Lord appointed seventy others, and sent them in pairs ahead of Him to every city and place where He Himself was going to come" (Luke 10:1).

Being able to share the load with someone else can be a great source of encouragement. In addition, teaming benefits from the pooled knowledge, experience, and skill sets of the partners involved. In 1 Corinthians 12, Paul acknowledged the importance of having variety in the miraculous gifts and ministries that were bestowed on believers in the early church. All originated from the same Spirit and the same Lord, uniting many as one: "For even as the body is one and yet has many members, and all the members of the body, though they are many, are one body, so also is Christ" (1 Cor. 12:12).

Although there were many different gifted individuals, they were all important contributors and all part of the same body—the Body of Christ, His Church.

For the body is not one member, but many. If the foot says, "Because I am not a hand, I am not a part of the body," it is not for this reason any the less a part of the body. And if the ear says, "Because I am not an eye, I am not a part of the body," it is not for this reason any the less a part of the body. If the whole body were an eye, where would the hearing be? If the whole were hearing, where would the sense of smell be? But now God has placed the members, each one of them, in the body, just as He desired. If they were all one member, where would the body be? But now there are many members, but one body. (1 Cor. 12:14–20)

Here, Paul describes the importance and advantage of having diversity in the body. It is the sum of the parts that make the whole. Without all of its parts, the body is incomplete. In his letter to the Ephesians, Paul explained what is necessary for the growth of the body. "From whom the whole body, being fitted and held together by what every joint supplies, according to the proper working of each individual part, causes the growth of the body for the building up of itself in love" (Eph. 4:16). The Body of Christ grows through what each individual supplies when all Christians are functioning, working together and contributing as they should.

Church evangelism is a group effort where each and every member has an important part to play in seeking and saving the lost. Although the ways people contribute to that mission may vary depending upon their talents and abilities, there a role for everyone. The challenge is identifying and accepting that role.

CHAPTER

Lighting Up the World

"THIS IS THE MESSAGE WE HAVE HEARD FROM HIM AND announce to you, that God is Light, and in Him there is no darkness at all" (1 John 1:5). Throughout the Bible, light and darkness are used consistently to contrast the difference between good and evil.

> But the path of the righteous is like the light of dawn, that shines brighter and brighter until the full day. The way of the wicked is like darkness; They do not know over what they stumble. (Prov. 4:18–19)

As Jesus began His ministry, He made it clear that He came to overcome evil with good, bringing light to a dark world.

> Then Jesus again spoke to them, saying, "I am the Light of the world; he who follows Me will not

walk in the darkness, but will have the Light of life." (John 8:12)

I have come as Light into the world, so that everyone who believes in Me will not remain in darkness. (John 12:46)

Whether aware of it or not, we are involved in spiritual warfare. It is a fight between good and evil, and we must each choose a side. God, our Creator and Heavenly Father, wants humankind to be holy as He is holy (1 Pet. 1:14–16), but from the beginning, the devil has schemed to thwart the efforts of God using lies and deception. It is only through Jesus that victory can be attained.

Put on the full armor of God, so that you will be able to stand firm against the schemes of the devil. For our struggle is not against flesh and blood, but against the rulers, against the powers, against the world forces of this darkness, against the spiritual forces of wickedness in the heavenly places. (Eph. 6:11–12)

The one who practices sin is of the devil; for the devil has sinned from the beginning. The Son of God appeared for this purpose, to destroy the works of the devil. (1 John 3:8)

You are of your father the devil, and you want to do the desires of your father. He was a murderer from the beginning, and does not stand in the truth because there is no truth in him. Whenever

> he speaks a lie, he speaks from his own nature, for
> he is a liar and the father of lies. (John 8:44)

Through the sacrifice of Jesus, obedient believers can obtain God's forgiveness and maintain holiness by abandoning darkness to walk in the light.

> If we say that we have fellowship with Him and yet
> walk in the darkness, we lie and do not practice the
> truth; but if we walk in the Light as He Himself is
> in the Light, we have fellowship with one another,
> and the blood of Jesus His Son cleanses us from
> all sin. (1 John 1:6–7)

As Christians, our goal is to light up the world, and there are two ways to do it.

1. **By example.** Walk in the light and be a light for others to see.
2. **By making more lights.** Share the gospel and grow the Body of Christ.

Jesus called His disciples the light of the world. By setting the right example, living a holy life and performing good works, Christians can brighten the lives around them and bring glory to the Heavenly Father (Matt. 5:14–16). We must never underestimate the impact a godly person can have on the lives of struggling souls searching for a better way.

The apostle Paul provided a further explanation of what it means to be children of light and how to keep those lights shining brightly.

> For you were formerly darkness, but now you are Light in the Lord; walk as children of Light (for the fruit of the Light consists in all goodness and righteousness and truth), trying to learn what is pleasing to the Lord. Do not participate in the unfruitful deeds of darkness, but instead even expose them. (Eph. 5:8–11)

As Christians commit themselves to God's Word, their lights become brighter and their influence greater, but there is even more that can be done to light up the world. God's people can make more lights by proclaiming the message of Jesus, just as the apostle Peter declared (1 Pet. 2:9).

Although one light can brighten a dark room, many can light up the world. Leaving the darkness to walk in the light is only the first step to be taken. The next is for those Christians to lead others out of the darkness into the light. That is evangelism, and the gospel is the light we are to share.

These principles of evangelism are clearly seen in Paul's conversion as Jesus directed him to become a minister leading people from darkness into the light, turning them from Satan to God by offering salvation through faith in Jesus.

> But get up and stand on your feet; for this purpose I have appeared to you, to appoint you a minister and a witness not only to the things which you have seen, but also to the things in which I will appear to you; rescuing you from the Jewish people and from the Gentiles, to whom I am sending you, to open their eyes so that they may turn from darkness to light and from the dominion of Satan

to God, that they may receive forgiveness of sins and an inheritance among those who have been sanctified by faith in Me. (Acts 26:16–18)

Christians are to follow Paul's lead "Be imitators of me, just as I also am of Christ" (1 Cor. 11:1).

There is a biblical pattern for making more lights in the world, and it is found in the instructions Paul gave to Timothy.

You therefore, my son, be strong in the grace that is in Christ Jesus. The things which you have heard from me in the presence of many witnesses, entrust these to faithful men who will be able to teach others also. (2 Tim. 2:1–2)

Paul was a teacher and a mentor. Not only did he encourage Timothy to continue walking in the light (2 Tim. 3:14–15), but he also instructed Timothy to take what he had learned and pass it on to other faithful Christians. Notice, however, the process was not to stop there. These faithful Christians then were to become teachers and mentors—making more Timothys.

This is a model for an evangelistic chain. Christians are to share the gospel, making new converts who in turn are to become teachers teaching others to do the same. That leads to a self-propagating sequence whereby Christians make Christians who make Christians. If every new convert is mentored to share the gospel with others (i.e., to become an ambassador for Christ), then the supply of evangelists will continue to grow in a never-ending fashion, and Jesus's request to "beseech the Lord of the harvest to send out workers into His harvest" (Matt. 9:38) will be fulfilled.

How powerful is this approach? Consider two examples. In the first, Christian A decides to pursue evangelism by teaching the gospel and converting one precious soul per year. That convert is then welcomed into the church while Christian A pursues another prospect over the next year. This cycle continues year after year. In the second, Christian B not only commits to teaching the gospel and converting one person to Christ each year but also agrees to mentor that individual. Specifically, each new convert is taught to become evangelistic and to continue Christ's mission by following the same pattern of teaching, converting, and likewise mentoring one new person each year.

Now examine the outcomes produced by these two cases. Christian A adds one new convert to the Body of Christ each year, so after twenty years, twenty new Christians have been produced. Christian B not only shares the gospel but mentors the new converts to become evangelistic—teaching and mentoring others to do likewise. In the first year, Christian B also produces one convert, the same number as Christian A. However, at the end of the second year, Christian A has produced a total of two converts while Christian B has three. What is different? Christians A and B are each producing one new Christian a year, but the converts of Christian B are also each generating one new Christian a year. This difference grows dramatically in subsequent years, as can be seen in Table 1.

After twenty years, Christian B will be responsible for bringing over one million new Christians into the Lord's Church, whereas Christian A will have produced only twenty. Both saved souls, but one effort grew enormously. The difference arises from the fact that Christian B followed the model found in Paul's instructions to Timothy. Christian B taught the gospel message and mentored new converts, equipping them to embrace Christ's mission of seeking and saving the lost. It is Christians making Christians who make Christians!

Some other interesting possibilities can be derived from Table 1. Suppose each Christian produced only one convert every two years. How would that alter the results? In that case, it would take twice as long to achieve the outcomes discussed in the previous paragraph. Forty years would be required for Christian B to generate over a million converts. That is still a great outcome. Now suppose instead of just one Christian B, there were ten Christian evangelists following the same model of teaching and mentoring one new convert every year. What would that do? That would produce ten times the result, making over ten million new Christians after just twenty years.

These are amazing numbers! Imagine the impact that could be obtained by harnessing and focusing the excitement, passion, and energy of new converts who have just been saved. What a marvelous time to encourage and help these babes in Christ reach out to others they care about with the saving message of Jesus! Sadly, the Lord's Church often misses this opportunity by not doing a good job of mentoring new Christians.

Table 1. A comparison of the exponential growth of Christians produced when (A) an evangelist converts one person per year and (B) an evangelist converts but also mentors new converts to become evangelistic themselves.

Year	Total Number of Converts Produced	
	Teaching one person per year (Christian A)	Teaching and mentoring evangelistic converts (Christian B)
1	1	1
2	2	3
3	3	7
4	4	15
5	5	31
10	10	1,023
15	15	32,767
20	20	1,048,575

CHAPTER

Making Disciples

THE DIRECTIVE TO GO INTO ALL THE WORLD PREACHING THE gospel was issued by Jesus to His apostles in what has become known as the Great Commission.

> And He said to them, "Go into all the world and preach the gospel to all creation. He who has believed and has been baptized shall be saved; but he who has disbelieved shall be condemned." (Mark 16:15–16)

> And Jesus came up and spoke to them, saying, "All authority has been given to Me in heaven and on earth. Go therefore and make disciples of all the nations, baptizing them in the name of the Father and the Son and the Holy Spirit, teaching them to observe all that I commanded you; and lo, I am

with you always, even to the end of the age." (Matt. 28:18–20)

The proclamation of the gospel went forth from Jerusalem on the Day of Pentecost, and some 3,000 souls were added to the Lord's Church (Acts 2:41). So began the mission of evangelism. Although Jesus commanded the apostles to go forth making disciples of all nations by baptizing and teaching them, He did not specify how His followers were to go about sharing the gospel with the whole world. That was left in the hands of capable men who were empowered by the Holy Spirit.

The book of Acts records many subsequent conversion accounts as the good news of Jesus was taught in a variety of different settings. Peter preached before large crowds on the Day of Pentecost (Acts 2:14–36) and again at the Portico of Solomon following the healing of the lame man at the Beautiful Gate of the temple (Acts 3). Persecuted Christians who were driven from Jerusalem began preaching the Word wherever they went (Acts 8:1–4). The Holy Spirit directed Philip to an individual study with an Ethiopian eunuch traveling on a desert road (Acts 8:26–39), and Peter traveled to Caesarea, where he taught Cornelius along with family and friends who had gathered to hear the message (Acts 10:23–48).

In modern times, congregations have continued to spread the Word of God through a variety of approaches, including:

- **personal evangelism**, individual Bible studies conducted by Christians
- **gospel meetings or tent meetings**, community events inviting evening and weekend crowds to attend presentations of the gospel

- **pulpit preaching**, dedicated church sermons offering an invitation to obey the gospel
- **lectureships**, congregational seminars hosting a variety of speakers addressing evangelistic topics or themes
- **door-knocking campaigns**, house to house invitations issued by members to attend special church meetings or Bible studies
- **Jule Miller filmstrips**, home Bible studies conducted by church members using slide projections and recordings
- **television or radio broadcasts** featuring gospel lessons
- **phone campaigns** inviting households to Bible studies or worship services
- **mailings and flyers (handbills)** promoting congregational events or meetings
- **bus programs** enrolling and transporting children and families to Church services
- **Bible class promotions** inviting classmates and families to Bible classes
- **Bible correspondence courses**, Bible studies conducted through the mail
- **DVDs, tapes, or cassettes**, video and audio presentations broadly distributed (e.g., World Video Bible School)

Although God's message remains the same, our society and the times we live in have changed. The rise in crime, home invasions, telemarketing, robocalls, and identity theft have made people suspicious of unsolicited phone calls and home visits. Cold calls, door knocking, and blanket mailings are often viewed as a nuisance or perhaps even a safety threat. Consequently, some past approaches to evangelism are no longer as effective.

There is another phenomenon that has transpired with the

changing generations. Attention spans have decreased. Time is precious, and people are more impatient in wanting to exchange information and ideas quickly, as is readily apparent in political and advertising campaigns that make use of sound bites, punch lines, and talking points. The time frame within which it is possible to capture an individual's attention and interest is shrinking rapidly.

Perhaps because of shortened attention spans and the desire to get in and out quickly, personal interactions are gradually being replaced by more impersonal electronic communications. With the rise in the popularity of smartphones, more and more people communicate by texting. Voice exchanges, if they occur, are often short and sweet or relayed as voice mail. People-to-people contacts are becoming rarer and are being replaced by social media apps like Instagram, Facebook, Twitter, TikTok, and YouTube.

With the explosion of the internet, computer networks span the globe, making information available to literally billions of people through the World Wide Web. Blogs, emails, and video conferencing have provided practically instantaneous links among people, and these resources are widely accessible through smartphones, tablets, laptops, and desktop computers, as well as smart televisions and even watches.

Through websites, interested parties can readily access articles, podcasts, audio, and videos that are available twenty-four hours a day, seven days a week, in the privacy of their own home. This presence provides a tremendous opportunity to share the good news of Jesus. Website evangelism is well suited to the changes in lifestyle and personal interactions that have occurred in the twenty-first century.

CHAPTER

Website Evangelism

Sharing the good news of Jesus is something all Christians can and should be doing. In fact, the apostle Paul clearly stated that Christians are to be "ambassadors for Christ, as though God were making an appeal through us" (2 Cor. 5:20). The question most often raised is "How do I do that?"

There are two critical elements in evangelism, and they were identified by Jesus when He said that He had come to seek and to save the lost (Luke 19:10). First, one must initiate contact, establishing a connection with someone who needs to hear the saving message of Jesus. This is the seeking part—reaching out to the lost. The second part is teaching the gospel, sharing the truth that convicts the hearts of sinners and leads them to repentance and obedience, in turn bringing salvation through the forgiveness of sins.

The simple fact is that Christians have different God-given talents and abilities. Some Christians are outgoing and quite comfortable doing the seeking part of evangelism but may need help with the teaching. Others are great teachers but have a hard time meeting and connecting with people to teach. These gaps in knowledge and experience very often are the things that make Christians shy away from their God-given mission to evangelize. Fortunately, there are ways to deal with such shortcomings.

While seeking and saving are both important aspects of the mission, Christians don't have to be proficient in both. Deficiencies can be overcome by teaming with someone who has a complementary skill set. The difficulty often is finding the right partner. Being taught and mentored by an experienced evangelist is another way to fill the gaps and learn how to engage in personal evangelism. Mentoring was introduced and discussed in chapter 10 as the next step in the spiritual growth and development of new converts. Although teaming and mentoring are both excellent ways to prepare Christians to become ambassadors for Christ, frequently there is a shortage of talent available to serve as partners, teachers, and mentors. This is particularly true in smaller congregations.

What else can be done to prepare and equip Christians for their mission in evangelism? Here is where a website can help. Through the technology of the internet, people everywhere can access training and teaching materials at any time without leaving home. A website can serve as the teacher and mentor, offering instruction and guidance from experienced Christians. Not only can a website help fill in knowledge gaps, but it also can provide Bible study outlines and presentation materials capable of doing the actual teaching. The website at www.TheTruthTransforms.com was designed to achieve these very things.

CHAPTER

Using the Website
TheTruthTransforms.com

ONE OF THE GREATEST WORRIES FACED IN PERSONAL evangelism is the fear of making mistakes—doing or saying something that undermines the effort to save a lost soul. I recall these concerns from my own first Bible study. I felt alone, uncomfortable, and my demeanor was not as relaxed as I would have liked. However, these feeling changed after conducting more Bible studies. I grew spiritually and learned from my mistakes and interactions with people who had been raised under different religious backgrounds. After years as a Christian, I finally understood the need and accepted the importance of continuing Christ's mission. That zeal motivated me to create TheTruthTransforms.com website so I can share the things that I have learned and used to teach the good news of Jesus.

TheTruthTransforms.com features multimedia resources

designed to make, foster, and grow disciples of Jesus Christ, including articles, videos, audio, Bible study outlines, a teaching template, and presentation slides with three objectives:

1. making the good news of Jesus readily available to anyone interested in learning the biblical truth about Christianity and what it means to be saved
2. providing both training and teaching resources for Christians who want to learn how to engage in personal evangelism by sharing the saving message of Jesus with those who need to hear it
3. introducing Bible-based study materials and presentations to encourage and foster spiritual awareness and growth

For Christians who are interested in personal evangelism, there is an entire section of the website devoted to evangelism and teaching the gospel. Its goal is to fill in knowledge and experience gaps by providing the basic training and teaching materials needed to equip Christians to fulfill their mission as ambassadors for Christ.

Training for Evangelism

No one wants to take on a task without being prepared properly to meet the challenges ahead. This is particularly true in personal evangelism. Two questions immediately come to mind:

1. How do I get started?
2. How do I lead a Bible study?

The answers to these two questions are addressed in two articles found in the "Evangelism: Teaching the Gospel" section of the website. Abstracts summarizing the content of these two articles follow. The articles can be downloaded and printed directly from the website and also are available as audio for those who might like to hear presentations. Both articles are reproduced in their entirety as later chapters of this book.

"How to Initiate Bible Studies" (chapter 14) emphasizes the importance of and need for personal evangelism and provides specific instructions on how to get started. It includes valuable information about how to develop and improve essential people skills such as overcoming the fear of meeting and talking to new people. There are also suggestions for ways to develop prospects for Bible studies and examples of how to recognize and pursue opportunities that can lead to teaching people the gospel of Jesus. These techniques are designed to help Christians learn how to seek the lost.

"Recommendations for Bible Study Leaders" (chapter 16) contains a detailed list of suggestions about things to do and things not to do when leading a Bible study. For people who have never taught one-on-one or in a small group, conducting a Bible study can be a stressful undertaking. These helpful hints are provided to put teachers more at ease and to avoid some of the distractions that can make the Bible study less effective. This article focuses on the techniques of teaching. A discussion of the subject matter to be taught is covered in the next section.

Teaching Resources for Evangelism

When presenting the gospel message, it is very important to use teaching time wisely. After all, there may be only one opportunity to meet with an individual. What are the most important things to say and how do you say them? Although people may approach the topic differently, it is useful to have a starting point serving as a guide for individuals who want to learn what to teach. With that in mind, the TruthTransforms website provides an overview article, a teaching template, and presentations all designed for teaching the gospel in personal evangelism. These materials are described subsequently and are available through the links in the "Evangelism: Teaching the Gospel" section of the website. The teaching template and the article describing its content are presented in chapters 17 and 18.

The Teaching Template (chapter 17) is an illustrated outline for a personal Bible study to last just over an hour. This template has the dual purposes of serving both as a teacher's guide (i.e., set of notes) for Bible study leaders and as a learning handout for Bible students. It presents the good news of Jesus through five Pillars of Truth that underlie the Christian faith. The template can be downloaded directly from the website for printing and distribution as needed.

"The Good News of Jesus Christ" (chapter 18) provides an explanation of the five Pillars of Truth referenced in the presentation of the gospel outlined in the Teaching Template. The intent of the article is twofold:

1. to equip Bible study leaders with the background and explanations needed to present the gospel using the Teaching Template as a guide
2. to provide students with a concise written summary of God's plan to save humankind through Jesus

This article is useful both for teachers who want to learn what to say when teaching from the template and for students who want to read the account for themselves. Audio of the article is also available for people who prefer to listen to a presentation.

Teaching Template Presentations are multimedia resources for Bible study leaders who would like to allow the website to do the actual teaching from the illustrated teaching template. These can be accessed in video, audio, or slideshow formats. The first presentation introduces the five Pillars of Truth which form the foundation of the Christian faith. It is followed by five individual presentations describing each of the topics individually, corresponding to the subject matter illustrated in the five horizontal panels of the teaching template. A seventh presentation discusses what comes next for new Christians.

With these teaching presentations, personal evangelism can be conducted by simply meeting with an individual and allowing the website to do the teaching by playing a website video or audio on a smartphone, tablet, or laptop computer. For study leaders who want to take a more active role, the presentation slides can be shown and discussed with the student. Interested parties who prefer to study alone can access any of these multimedia teaching resources at their convenience as often as they like.

Additional Bible-Based Resources

For teachers who want to do additional preparation, or for anyone seeking a greater understanding of the Christian faith, the website offers other study aids.

Articles. In addition to the articles already mentioned, there is a separate section on the website presenting articles on a range of topics. These topics are chosen to explain the role truth plays in transforming lives and to provide meaning, purpose, and perspective to human life and its struggles.

"The Message and Mission of Jesus." This audio series

consists of an introduction followed by ten lessons, providing just over five and a half hours of recordings. As the title suggests, it covers the message and mission of Jesus, with a thorough overview of the basis for the Christian faith beginning at Creation and extending to the cross and establishment of the Church.

Study Outlines. The study outlines are ideal for building the faith of new converts or serving as curriculum for a congregation's weekly Bible classes. The series, entitled The Foundations of Christianity, covers three topics: The Gospel of Jesus, The Church, and Christian Worship. Each topical set of outlines contains sufficient content to support a typical thirteen-week series of Bible classes, each lasting forty-five minutes. The Gospel of Jesus covers the same material found in "The Message and Mission of Jesus" audio series.

Gospel Meetings YouTube Channel. These are video links to sermons I delivered at Church services and gospel meetings. The lessons focus on presentations of the gospel and personal evangelism.

Devotions YouTube Channel. These are video links to presentations of Bible lessons on a variety of topics designed to teach and encourage those who want to hear more about the wisdom the Bible has to offer.

The Truth Transforms YouTube Channel. These are links to videos addressing topics about God, Creation, science, and the spiritual realm. They are designed to appeal to individuals searching for the truth about life.

Books. The website also lists my books, which are available for purchase through links to my publisher, WestBow Press, or online retailers such as Amazon, Barnes & Noble, or Christianbook.

A Debt I Cannot Pay is a thorough study of God's plan to save

His people. If you are familiar with *Muscle and a Shovel* written by Michael Shank, then you may realize that *A Debt I Cannot Pay* is a book that Randall Edges was sure to have on his bookshelf. It is an inspiring and insightful spiritual guidebook and Bible commentary that focuses on the deep and abiding relationship God has with us, His children, and how He gave so much in His Son in order for us to be with Him forever without sin and for eternity. It explores God's plan of salvation as presented also in "The Message and Mission of Jesus" audio series.

In *Continuing Christ's Mission*, I make the case for Christian evangelism in the twenty-first century by addressing obstacles and outlining new opportunities for sharing the gospel and equipping Christians to become ambassadors for Christ. Jesus commanded His disciples to "Go into all the world and preach the gospel." That was the Great Commission of two thousand years ago, but is it still viable in today's politically correct world of religious diversity? This book introduces training and teaching materials for evangelism and self-study in conjunction with TheTruthTransforms.com website.

These two books form a teaching series designed to equip every Christian with the background, knowledge, and resources needed to spread the good news of Jesus. Taken together, these books provide congregations with the instructional content for a class on personal evangelism, ideal for recruiting and equipping members to take on a larger role in sharing the gospel with others.

Personal Evangelism for Everyone

Sharing the good news of Jesus is something all Christians should be doing. What holds many people back is not knowing what to do. The fact is, there is a role for everyone.

Through <u>TheTruthTransforms.com,</u> everyone has access to a qualified teacher and mentor. The website can do the teaching through videos, audio, slideshows, and articles, if this material can be placed into the hands of the people who need to hear the Truth. That is where everyone can help—by connecting people to the website.

In this electronic age, the internet has become widely accessible through smartphones, tablets, laptop computers, desktop computers, and smart televisions and watches. The website provides a means to get the good news of Jesus into the hands of literally billions of people. To do that, however, people must be made aware of its existence. That means individual Christians must be willing to get involved by sharing the web address at <u>www. TheTruthTransforms.com</u> with other people. Here are some easy ways to do it:

- Post links on social media platforms, newsletters, publications, newspapers, journals.
- Promote the website on Facebook, YouTube, Twitter, Instagram, and other social media.
- Email the information to your contact lists.
- Add the website address to your email signatures.
- Share with friends and family by means of cards, letters, phone calls, and texts.
- Post the web address on a congregation's bulletin and website.
- Make business cards for evangelistic outreach and distribute them, including the web address, <u>www. TheTruthTransforms.com.</u>
- Recruit Christians to engage in evangelism by giving them a copy of this book.

- Give a copy of *A Debt I Cannot Pay* to someone who needs to hear the gospel.
- Reference this book chapter or go to <u>TheTruthTransforms.com</u> and download the article "How to Use the Website in Personal Evangelism." Use the article to build a team of evangelists. Distribute it to people to excite their interest and solicit their help.
- Be creative and use individual initiative to find ways to share the gospel using the website resources.

It is important for Christians to continue Christ's mission of preaching the gospel to the whole world. Jesus was willing to die for that cause. The question is, "What are we willing to do?"

CHAPTER

How to Initiate
Bible Studies

WHAT WAS TRUE TWO THOUSAND YEARS AGO IS STILL TRUE
today. More harvest workers are needed (Matt. 9:37–38). Clearly,
the world needs to hear the saving message of Jesus Christ.
Christianity offers hope and can bring peace, comfort, and
encouragement to struggling souls. A true disciple must be willing
to "deny himself, and take up his cross and follow Me" (Mark 8:34).
So said Jesus. That means doing as He did—seeking and saving
the lost.

The message has been revealed. The challenges lie in
developing more evangelists and reaching the people who need
to hear the truth about Christianity. Personal evangelism is an
endeavor that many Christians dread because it means engaging
in spiritual discussions on a very personal level. Although meeting
new people comes naturally for those with outgoing personalities,

many others find it uncomfortable and intimidating. Fortunately, these people skills can be learned, and that is the first challenge to be met.

Overcoming the Fear of Meeting New People

As with any new undertaking, the more often you do it, the easier it becomes. But where is the ideal place to practice meeting people you don't know, and do it in a safe atmosphere among kind, forgiving people? The obvious answer is among your own church family. If you are like most Christians, you regularly attend worship services in a congregation where you have a circle of close friends. However, there are probably other members whom you do not know well personally. Widening your sphere of relationships takes time, especially in a larger congregation, but this should be the goal.

Therein lies the opportunity for personal growth in learning how to become comfortable meeting "strangers." It may be as simple as approaching an unfamiliar face and saying, "Hi, I don't believe we have met. My name is ——." That is all that is needed to get things started. Their response will provide the lead to follow. Questions like "How long have you attended?" or "Where are you from?" are natural opportunities to learn more and continue the dialogue.

To build on new relationships, make notes—actually write down the names of the people you meet along with a few details to help you remember what you have learned about them. Then make an effort to speak to them again the following week and in the weeks beyond. Each time you do, build on prior conversations. For example, "What brought you here from Ohio?" Over time, you will discover things that you share in common, and your friendship will grow. As your circle of friends increases, you will become more and more comfortable interacting with new people.

Other church opportunities arise when people go public with prayer requests or bulletin announcements. In those cases, you have the advantage of knowing the person's name and needs in advance. An introduction and acknowledgment from you can not only build a new relationship but also impart encouragement. Making that contact nurtures your own spiritual growth and can be a source of great personal satisfaction in rendering comfort and aid to others.

Weekly Evangelistic Opportunities

Christians assemble on the first day of the week to remember the sacrifice of Jesus, worship God, grow spiritually, and enjoy fellowship with one another. Unfortunately, many members spend most of that time in the company of their family and closest friends. By human nature, we tend to stay in our own comfort zones instead of reaching out to meet strangers and make new acquaintances. But this is a missed opportunity and a failure that can lead to the reputation of being an unfriendly congregation.

In fact, most congregations have visitors who show up for worship services. Perhaps these are travelers passing through, but sometimes they are people looking for a church home or wanting to see what the church is all about. These folks often are seated in the rear of the auditorium or back of the class where they can depart quickly if they feel uncomfortable or unwelcome. A friendly greeting and acknowledgment from an attentive church member can have a huge impact.

This is an excellent chance for members to gain experience in meeting people who have already shown an interest in Christianity. Making them feel welcome and getting to know them better are ways to show God's love that may lead naturally to a Bible study. It is a perfect opportunity to teach by answering questions from those who want to learn more about the congregation, its beliefs, and its worship. This is what personal evangelism is all about.

Often there are greeters in a congregation assigned to welcome guests and visitors. Joining such teams is an excellent way to gain experience in meeting more people. Whether as part of the official greeters or not, identifying and welcoming visitors should be a high priority among all church members. Unfortunately, it is not. Can you imagine the impact of having dozens and dozens of members greet each and every visitor? Bible studies would increase, the church would grow, and the reputation of the Lord's congregation would flourish.

Here are some things every Christian can do:

- Welcome visitors and see whether they have attended worship services before. If they have not, ask "Would you like to learn more about the church?"
- Distribute visitors' welcome packets and bulletins.
- Introduce visitors to other members.
- Sit with visitors so they do not feel alone.
- Take visitors to a Bible class and show them around the facility.
- Give visitors your personal contact information. You might even want to print cards similar in format to business cards.
- Follow up with visitors and invite them back.
- Nurture the contact and allow the relationship to blossom.

These are evangelistic steps that can be undertaken each week as the church assembles for worship and Bible classes. But don't overlook other occasions midweek.

A large part of success in personal evangelism comes from recognizing opportunities and acting on them. To do that we must raise our awareness by remembering two important principles in building new relationships and initiating Bible studies:

1. People do not care how much you know until they know how much you care.
2. God answers prayers.

We seek to save the lost because we love them and want what's best for them. That sentiment must be apparent in all our interactions. We must be genuine. Although we sometimes feel alone in our pursuits, God is always with us. Prayers are powerful, and God is able to provide us with strength and wisdom filling in the gaps if only we will ask.

Following are suggestions for ways to make the most out of opportunities to share the gospel.

Build on existing relationships.

- Visit family or friends in their homes and invite them into your home.
- Have a meal together.
- Look for areas of common interest and talk about those things.
- Watch for openings that lead to spiritual discussions: "I notice that you are wearing a cross. Are you a Christian?" or "I see you have a Bible on your bookshelf. Do you enjoy Bible studies?"

- Let people see your faith. Make it known.
- Offer to pray for their needs and concerns.
- Pray before meals together.
- Invite them to attend Bible classes and worship services with you.

Watch for individuals and families in crisis or undergoing life-changing events.

- When people are experiencing life events such as death, sickness, auto accidents, personal struggles, or new births, initiate visits.
- Offer encouragement. Send cards, emails, or texts. Pray together. Nurture interactions.
- Offer to help by babysitting, washing dishes or clothes, shopping, or preparing meals.
- Welcome newcomers in the community.

Follow up with new converts.

- Harness and focus the excitement of new Christians. Strike while the iron is hot.
- Ask them, "Now whom do you know that needs to hear the gospel?"
- Offer to go with them to help lead a Bible study. Be a mentor.

When dining out in public, pray before your meals.

- Ask your server if they have any prayer requests.
- Leave a note or card promoting TheTruthTransforms. com—the website offers many Bible study resources.

Be observant in public settings.

- While standing in line at the store or an event, ask people, "How are you doing today?" If they say "Great," you can say, "Me too! Isn't God wonderful? I feel so blessed. Would you like to join me for worship services or a Bible study?" If they say "Terrible," you can say, "I've been there too, but I've found that God and His people can be a great help in tough times. Would you like to learn more about how?"
- Look for ways to inject God and religion into conversations. For example, say "What a beautiful day God has given us!" Gauge the reaction and turn it into a further discussion or an invitation to study or attend worship.
- Note subtle religious words or phrases people use and follow up on them. Respond to a "God bless you" following a sneeze by perhaps saying, "He already has in many ways! Would you like to hear how? How about you?"

Opportunities are there to reach people, but often we simply do not recognize them.

- Be alert in looking and listening for openings.
- Train yourself to detect and react—this takes practice and experience.
- Enlisting a second set of eyes and ears (such as a spouse) can increase your awareness.
- When and if an opportunity is missed, learn from it and do a better job next time.

When people you invite agree to attend congregational worship services or Bible classes, follow up.

- Make arrangements to meet and welcome them at the door.
- Be a gracious host.
- Introduce them to other members.
- Sit with them.
- Take them to Bible class and show them around the facility.

Make the most of each opportunity.

- Have business cards printed with contact information and a spiritual message or opportunity to study (e.g., the studies available at TheTruthTransforms.com).
- Carry the cards with you at all times and hand them to those you talk to.
- Even if they don't attend worship or Bible classes, they might study through a website.

Finally, do not get discouraged.

- Some people will not be interested in what the Bible has to say. That is their choice, based on the free will God has given to them.
- Pray for them, but never allow that experience to keep you from continuing to do the right thing.
- As Christians, our obligation is to be evangelistic, sharing the good news of Jesus and equipping people with the facts needed to make an informed decision.
- Ultimately, people must decide for themselves what they will do with Jesus.

CHAPTER

Often Missed
Opportunities

As MENTIONED IN EARLIER CHAPTERS, THERE ARE TWO PARTS
to evangelism. The first is seeking the lost—making that important
connection with individuals who need to hear the gospel. The
second is sharing the message of Jesus—equipping people with
the facts needed to make an informed decision about their eternal
future.

Christians belong to the Body of Christ and are charged
with continuing Christ's mission, but that does not mean we all
must serve in the same capacity. Individual roles may differ and
often are complementary, working together as a team to soften
an honest heart and make it more receptive to the message of
Jesus.

> What then is Apollos? And what is Paul? Servants
> through whom you believed, even as the Lord

gave opportunity to each one. I planted, Apollos watered, but God was causing the growth. So then neither the one who plants nor the one who waters is anything, but God who causes the growth. Now he who plants and he who waters are one; but each will receive his own reward according to his own labor. For we are God's fellow workers; you are God's field, God's building. (1 Cor. 3:5–9)

Christians serve not for their personal glory but out of love as God's fellow workers, delivering the good news of Jesus offering salvation to lost souls.

In Matthew 13:3–23, Jesus uses the parable of the sower to describe the differences in how people receive the Word of God. He made the comparison to the yield obtained when a sower planted seed in different environments: beside the road, on rocky places, among thorns, and on good soil. Only the good soil yielded a bountiful crop. This is like the honest heart who hears the Word, understands it, and bears fruit. By showing interest and concern for the lives of others through words and deeds, Christians can effectively create the good soil needed to bear spiritual fruit.

In the course of our day-to-day activities and interactions with people on the first day of the week, we encounter many ways to promote the cause of Christ. However, they are often overlooked—not on purpose, but because we have not trained ourselves properly to recognize and take advantage of the opportunities before us to create that good soil.

Making the Most of Our Opportunities

There are things that all Christians can do to demonstrate God's love to the people around them. Sometimes showing people that you care is all it takes to open a door to a future Bible study. This is part of what Jesus describes in Matthew 5:16: "Let your light shine before men in such a way that they may see your good works, and glorify your Father who is in heaven."

What attitudes and behaviors contribute to the mission of evangelism?

Attitudes

- Be friendly, upbeat, and positive—no one likes a grouch or complainer.
- Be an encourager, lifting people up and supporting them during tough times.
- Nurture the contacts you make. Follow up and show interest in people.

Behaviors

- Socialize—interact with people and build relationships.
- Take someone out to eat.
- Invite people into your home.
- Be benevolent and give to those in need, financially or by rendering aid (including everyday tasks such as washing dishes, cleaning house, and doing laundry).
- Don't neglect family ties, including family members or friends of family who have not obeyed the gospel.

What actions can you take to carry out the mission of evangelism?

Maintain focus.

- Look for ways to bring Christianity into conversations.
- Pray for wisdom and for people to study with.
- Share your observations and experiences with like-minded Christians.
- Learn from others.
- Don't be afraid to ask for help when you need it.

Support the work of the church.

- Distribute Bible tracts. Most congregations stock a supply.
- Invite guests to Bible class and worship on Sunday.
- Make a conscious effort to seek out visitors in Bible class and worship services. Greet them and introduce yourself. Make them feel welcome. Show them around the church facility.
- Sit with visitors in Bible class or worship services.
- Introduce visitors and guests to other members.
- Visit, email, or phone guests and visitors.
- Edify, encourage, and be a friend to new members and new converts.

Promote evangelism.

- Host a Bible study in your home—a study you teach or one taught by someone else.
- Invite folks to your home Bible study.
- Teach a Bible class at church.
- Mentor someone. Encourage and demonstrate how to be evangelistic.

- Build a team or support group for those interested in evangelism, and encourage others to participate.

Finally, share the website at <u>TheTruthTransforms.com</u> with others and encourage them to do the same. The various teaching and training materials—including articles, audio, videos, slides, and curriculum—are all designed to support teaching the gospel and edifying Christians.

CHAPTER

Recommendations for Bible Study Leaders

CHRISTIANS SHOULD BE WILLING AND ABLE TO ACCOUNT FOR their belief in Jesus and to do so lovingly and confidently expressing a conviction of the heart.

> Who is there to harm you if you prove zealous for what is good? But even if you should suffer for the sake of righteousness, you are blessed. And do not fear their intimidation, and do not be troubled, but sanctify Christ as Lord in your hearts, always being ready to make a defense to everyone who asks you to give an account for the hope that is in you, yet with gentleness and reverence. (1 Pet. 3:13–15)

But how does one do it? This chapter focuses on the technique or method of delivery, offering practical advice about how a Bible study should be conducted.

Personal evangelism can be stressful for people who have never conducted an individual Bible study. Many fear saying or doing something "wrong." To overcome such concerns, it is useful to consider suggestions from experienced evangelists describing things to do and things not to do when conducting a Bible study. These helpful hints can put teachers more at ease and help avoid some of the distractions that make personal evangelism less productive.

Agree in advance on the meeting details. Eliminate confusion and misunderstanding by clearly defining the important logistics.

- When will the study begin?
- Where will it be held? Your home? Their home? Church building? Neutral site?
- Who will be participating? Allow participants to invite others so they feel more comfortable: spouse, neighbor, friend. Be aware that they may invite a preacher or other church member to sit in.
- How long will the study last? Sixty to ninety minutes?
- How often will you meet? One time? Once a week for four weeks?

These details help you to prepare and let students know what to expect.

Define the scope of the study and establish ground rules. This is to be a Bible study examining the good news of Jesus Christ and providing an overview of Christianity, specifically discussing God's plan of salvation. That is the topic that spawned the study in the first place.

However, before proceeding, you must agree on the source of authority—where you go to establish the truth. There is nothing more frustrating than launching a study and discovering later that there is no basis for agreement. It's like trying to compete in a sporting event where everyone plays by their own rules. The result is utter chaos. It is critical for all parties to embrace the same standard of truth and adhere to it.

Any gospel study must adopt the Bible as the sole source of spiritual authority. This excludes religious traditions, human doctrines, and institutional creeds. All truth and disagreements must be settled based on what God has revealed in the text of the Bible.

If this agreement is not reached, then there is no basis for the study. However, disagreement on this point may create an opportunity for a different study—one establishing the authority of scriptures by examining evidence supporting the Bible as the inspired word of God.

Before delving into the biblical text, take time to get to know your students. Relationships are an important part of personal evangelism. Putting everyone at ease through a "warm-up" helps create an opportunity to exchange valuable background information.

- Inquire about religious backgrounds.
- Listen carefully and do not interrupt.
- If they profess to be a Christian, ask when and how they became one. This may identify future study topics and teaching opportunities.
- Briefly tell about your background as appropriate, but don't dwell on yourself. You are not the focus.
- Be open, candid, and earn their trust.
- Set a relaxing tone for the study.

Have a study plan. Bible study leaders should prepare in advance and know the topics they are going to cover. If someone agrees to give up their time to hear the gospel, the last thing they want is to be subjected to a meandering stream of incoherent scriptures.

- Know what material you want to cover and how you want to present it.
- Be organized and structured but not rigid in your delivery.
- Consider using the Teaching Template presented in chapter 17, further explained in chapter 18, "The Good News of Jesus Christ." This illustrated study guide can be downloaded from TheTruthTransforms.com.
- Allow for some flexibility based on student needs and questions.

Let the Bible do the teaching. Having agreed to adopt the Bible as the sole source of authority and truth in all spiritual matters, use it to tell the good news of Jesus. Make it clear that the message under discussion comes directly from the biblical text.

- Cite scripture by book, chapter, and verse to back up the points being made.
- Examine the biblical text together.
- Allow the student to see and read the text along with you.

When teaching, be gentle and kind—not quarrelsome. In agreeing to a study of the gospel, people are making themselves vulnerable. They are sharing personal beliefs, and some of the things they have accepted as truth may differ from biblical teaching. This can be a shock, raising defenses and closing ears.

- Be patient and loving.
- Listen to concerns.
- Be aware of the potential to hurt someone's feelings but never compromise the truth.
- If need be, allow time for the teaching to soak in.
- Remember, you are soul winning, not debating.

"The Lord's bond-servant must not be quarrelsome, but be kind to all, able to teach, patient when wronged, with gentleness correcting those who are in opposition, if perhaps God may grant them repentance leading to the knowledge of the truth, and they may come to their senses and escape from the snare of the devil, having been held captive by him to do his will." (2 Tim. 2:24–26)

Never utter the words "Well, I think ..." A gospel study should not focus on personal opinions. No individual commands perfect knowledge. God alone is the source of truth, and everyone can learn from what God has revealed in the Bible.

- Do not express your personal opinions as truth—we are interested only in what God says. Your opinions as the study leader are not important. The objective is to determine what God has revealed.
- Always draw from God's Word so you can confidently say "The Bible says ..." Then if there is a disagreement, it becomes a contrast between the personal opinion of the student and the Truth of what the Bible says.
- By relying on what the Bible says, you depersonalize and deescalate disagreements, preventing discussion from becoming an argument between you and them. Instead, it becomes a difference between what they think and what the Bible says.

Take time to pause for questions and allow new concepts to be understood. Because the Bible is so rich in truths, something new can be learned even when reading the same scriptures over and over. For inexperienced Bible students, the content can be overwhelming. For that reason, it is important to allow people time to digest new concepts and ask questions for clarification.

- Encourage students to ask questions if there is something they don't understand. Understanding what is said now prevents confusion later in the study.
- People learn by asking questions and finding answers.
- Questions help the study leader identify knowledge gaps and areas of confusion as well as potential topics for future study.
- Keep the questions focused on the subject at hand. Do not get sidetracked or totally bogged down on something far off topic.

Be sure to cover the planned lesson content. Never forget that the goal for the Bible study is to teach the good news of salvation through Jesus Christ so everyone can hear the truth, understand the risks, and make informed decisions for themselves.

- Do what you agreed to—cover the material you proposed.
- Have a definite lesson plan, adhere to it, and be sure to achieve the goal.
- You may only have one opportunity to meet or study with this person. Make it count.
- If they agreed to a single meeting to study the gospel, then be certain they leave knowing the dangers of sin, the gift of forgiveness, and how to obtain it.

Do not try to tackle topics that are too advanced, either for you as the study leader or for them as the student. We are all on a learning curve when it comes to Bible study. There is no shame in that, but we must be aware of our limitations and unafraid to confront them. Concepts that seem simple for one person may be very advanced for another. Our desire is not to pool ignorance but to gain truth.

- If you encounter questions on topics that you are unfamiliar with, freely admit it.
- Be willing to say the words "I don't know" to show that you are being honest and you are learning too.
- Assure them you will study to find biblical answers to things you don't know.
- Invite them to examine the Bible for themselves so you can compare notes later.
- Rather than dodging a difficult question altogether, suggest addressing that question or topic in a future study after this lesson is finished. This is particularly important if the answer to the question is not straightforward and requires a prolonged study or explanation. It is also appropriate if the answer to a question draws on knowledge well beyond what the student currently commands.
- Difficult questions may be a sign of great interest leading to additional study opportunities, but beware: they also may be an attempt to disrupt the study or change the subject.

Do not be discouraged if someone does not obey the gospel. God has given humanity free will, allowing us to make decisions for ourselves. Not everyone will believe and follow through.

- If someone turns away from the Truth, *do not take it personally!*
- They are not rejecting you—they are rejecting the Word.
- Regardless, we can continue to love them and pray for them. The seed will have been planted, and it may blossom in the future.
- Remember, Jesus, the Son of God, was rejected by many: "The one who listens to you listens to Me, and the one who rejects you rejects Me; and he who rejects Me rejects the One who sent Me." (Luke 10:16)

As Christians, our duty is to teach the truth about spiritual realities. God wants everyone to hear the truth. Sin is real. Souls are in jeopardy, but there is a path to salvation through Jesus.

- Our goal is to equip people with the facts needed to make an informed decision.
- However, the decision is theirs. We cannot force people to believe the truth.

When the study has completed, maintain contact with your students. Let them know you are always there for them and willing to meet, discuss, and support them.

- Help them take the next steps: obeying the gospel and living for Christ.
- Encourage fellowship with other Christians.
- Nurture their spiritual growth and development.

By doing all these things, you will be serving as ambassadors for Christ.

CHAPTER

A Teaching Template

CHAPTERS 14 AND 15 HAVE ADDRESSED SOME OF THE REQUISITE people skills and strategies for initiating Bible studies. Now the attention is shifted to the content of the study itself. There are three distinct challenges faced in personal evangelism:

1. connecting with people where they are, based on their current understanding of Christianity
2. gaining acceptance of the Bible as the sole source of authority and truth
3. overcoming religious traditions and human doctrines

Although these principles may seem obvious, to many people they are not. Individual backgrounds and upbringings can vary considerably. Often religious traditions and human doctrines must be unlearned and replaced by biblical truths. Opening the eyes of people to see beliefs that conflict with biblical teaching can be a painful process. Although it may be easier to present the gospel to someone who has little knowledge of the Christian faith, everyone needs to hear the truth.

So how should the gospel be presented? There is no single right answer to this question because so much depends on the background and understanding of the individuals involved. However, there are some general principles worth noting.

Rather than beginning a study by quarreling over known contentious issues, it is much better to start from common ground, allowing the Bible to make its own case for the truth. This depersonalizes conflicts by focusing attention on what God has revealed instead of dwelling on human doctrines and ideas people have been raised to believe.

To fully appreciate what God has done for humankind in the sacrifice of Jesus Christ, it is important to understand what it means to be saved and why salvation is necessary. Those answers come from five pillars of truth that form the basis of the Christian faith.

1. **Relationship and identity.** God is the Creator and Spirit Being who established a unique relationship with humanity by bestowing humans with an eternal spirit.
2. **The Bible: the source of truth.** The Bible is the sole source of spiritual authority through which God has revealed His divine nature and expectations to humankind.
3. **The problem of sin.** Sin is deadly, leading to spiritual death and being separated from God for eternity in Hell.
4. **God's gift of salvation.** The path to eternal life and a home in Heaven is made available only through the loving sacrifice of Jesus.

5. **Claiming God's gift of salvation.** God has given specific instructions regarding how to claim His gift of salvation and have fellowship restored through the forgiveness of sins.

These five pillars build the case for Christianity, systematically defining important spiritual truths and the outcomes that will affect all humans at the point of physical death. Breaking the subject matter into these subtopics is a convenient way to expose people to the essential tenets of the Christian faith. This exposure will reinforce the beliefs of some and challenge the faith of others. In both cases, it lays the groundwork for further discussion and learning opportunities.

This is also where a teaching template comes in handy. An illustrated study guide provides the teacher with an organized outline of the subject matter to keep the lesson on track. It also serves as a handout that can be given to the student for later reference and study.

An example of a teaching template constructed from the five pillars of truth is shown in Figure 1. It is divided into five horizontal panels, one for each pillar topic, containing bullet points, scriptures, and illustrations to aid in the presentation of the gospel.

Having a study outline is one thing, but being able to explain it clearly is another. The explanation for each of the five panels in the teaching template can be found in "The Good News of Jesus Christ" presented in chapter 18.

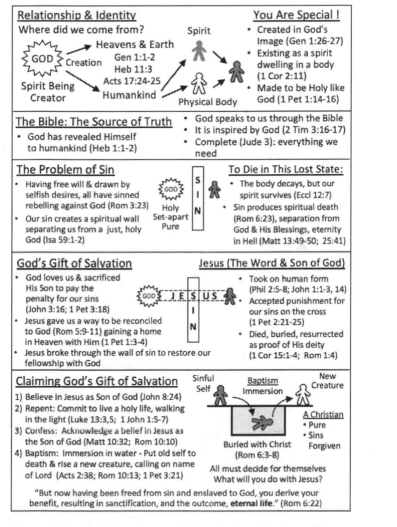

Relationship & Identity   You Are Special !

Where did we come from?   Spirit   • Created in God's
                                                  Image (Gen 1:26-27)
GOD — Creation → Heavens & Earth   • Existing as a spirit
                 Gen 1:1-2   dwelling in a body
                 Heb 11:3   (1 Cor 2:11)
Spirit Being → Humankind   • Made to be Holy like
Creator   Physical Body   God (1 Pet 1:14-16)

The Bible: The Source of Truth   • God speaks to us through the Bible
                                  • It is inspired by God (2 Tim 3:16-17)
• God has revealed Himself   • Complete (Jude 3): everything we
  to humankind (Heb 1:1-2)   need

The Problem of Sin   To Die in This Lost State:

• Having free will & drawn by   GOD S   • The body decays, but our
  selfish desires, all have sinned   I   spirit survives (Eccl 12:7)
  rebelling against God (Rom 3:23) Holy   • Sin produces spiritual death
                                    Set-apart N   (Rom 6:23), separation from
• Our sin creates a spiritual wall Pure   God & His Blessings, eternity
  separating us from a just, holy   in Hell (Matt 13:49-50; 25:41)
  God (Isa 59:1-2)

God's Gift of Salvation   Jesus (The Word & Son of God)

• God loves us & sacrificed   • Took on human form
  His Son to pay the   GOD JESUS   (Phil 2:5-8; John 1:1-3, 14)
  penalty for our sins   I   • Accepted punishment for
  (John 3:16; 1 Pet 3:18)   N   our sins on the cross
• Jesus gave us a way to be reconciled   (1 Pet 2:21-25)
  to God (Rom 5:9-11) gaining a home   • Died, buried, resurrected
  in Heaven with Him (1 Pet 1:3-4)   as proof of His deity
• Jesus broke through the wall of sin to restore our   (1 Cor 15:1-4; Rom 1:4)
  fellowship with God

Claiming God's Gift of Salvation   Sinful   Baptism   New
                                   Self   Immersion   Creature
1) Believe in Jesus as Son of God (John 8:24)
2) Repent: Commit to live a holy life, walking   A Christian
   in the light (Luke 13:3,5; 1 John 1:5-7)   • Pure
3) Confess: Acknowledge a belief in Jesus as   • Sins
   the Son of God (Matt 10:32; Rom 10:10)   Buried with Christ   Forgiven
4) Baptism: Immersion in water - Put old self to   (Rom 6:3-8)
   death & rise a new creature, calling on name   All must decide for themselves
   of Lord (Acts 2:38; Rom 10:13; 1 Pet 3:21)   What will you do with Jesus?

"But now having been freed from sin and enslaved to God, you derive your
benefit, resulting in sanctification, and the outcome, **eternal life**." (Rom 6:22)

Figure 1. A template for teaching the good news of Jesus

CHAPTER

The Good News of Jesus Christ

CHRISTIANS SHOULD BE WILLING TO SHARE THE GOOD NEWS of Jesus Christ. The motivation for preaching the gospel can be found in Paul's letter to the Romans, and it stems from the fact that sin leads to spiritual death (Rom. 6:23). Sooner or later sin claims everyone (Rom. 3:23), ultimately leading to an eternity separated from God in Hell. The good news is that there is a way out, and it is a free gift offered through Jesus.

Although sin is a threat facing all humanity, many people are unprepared to deal with it. Some are too wrapped up in the affairs of this world to care. Others are ignorant, either not knowing about the spiritual reality and threat from sin, or deceived by false teachings. Christians have a divine obligation to spread the truth so everyone can make informed decisions about their eternal future.

The truth Christians share is centered on the good news of Jesus Christ. It is the gospel—what the apostle Paul called the message of first importance involving the death, burial, and resurrection of Jesus, the Son of God (1 Cor. 15:1–4). However, without understanding the context surrounding these events, the significance of this message can be clouded and lost.

One of the major challenges of evangelism is presenting the gospel in a concise fashion with enough of the big picture and background for someone to comprehend and believe. Moreover, in many instances, this needs to be accomplished within the time frame of a meeting lasting about an hour, since the opportunity to continue discussions may vanish after that. While it is true an initial study may grow based on the questions and interest of the individual, that is not a certainty. With that in mind, the following sections are offered as an example of how to present the gospel, the good news of Jesus Christ, in a single session.

Introducing the Five Pillars of Truth

For many, the knowledge of Jesus comes from family tradition or what has been heard or read piecemeal in sermons, classes, and publications over the years. Often this is a jumbled collection of topics tainted by human doctrines confusing the actual message from God. Although the truth can be found in what God has revealed through the inspired text of the Bible, some are too intimidated by the Bible's volume and content to investigate things for themselves.

Christianity is not really hard to understand, nor does it require a blind faith. It is a logical accounting of reality that provides meaning and purpose to life and death. However, to grasp the big picture and fully appreciate the good news of Jesus Christ, it is important to lay the proper biblical foundation in an orderly fashion. That foundation is based on five key pillars of truth:

1. Relationship and identity
2. The Bible: the source of truth
3. The problem of sin
4. God's gift of salvation
5. Claiming God's gift of salvation

Pillar 1: Relationship and Identity

Christianity is all about a relationship between God and humankind, and to understand that relationship, it is important to know something about the parties involved. The Bible identifies God as the Spirit Being who created the heavens and the earth (Gen. 1:1–2, Heb. 11:3) and all things in them, including life itself (Acts 17:24–25).

Since the Creator existed when there was no creation, God clearly must dwell in another realm— i.e., a higher dimensional, spiritual realm that encompasses and transcends our physical domain. Among all the living creatures populating the earth, human beings are unique, having been created in the image and likeness of God (Gen. 1:26–27), possessing not only a physical body of flesh and blood but a spirit as well (1 Cor. 2:11).

That spiritual bond explains the great lengths to which God has gone to preserve fellowship with humanity. It might even be said that humans have a piece of God within. Being God's offspring makes us children of a Heavenly Father, one who loves us and wants us to be like Him—holy as God is holy (1 Pet. 1:14–16). God's desire is for humans to be "set apart," mimicking His purity and wholesomeness, separated from all unholy, evil things.

Pillar 2: The Bible, the Source of Truth

An objective, rational person can look at the vastness and complexity of the working universe and realize there must have been a Creator. However, unless that Creator chooses to reveal things affecting our relationship and existence, we have no way to acquire spiritual knowledge. Knowing that, God has revealed Himself to humankind over the course of time throughout the Patriarchal, Mosaic, and Christian Ages and has done so in many portions and many ways (Heb. 1:1–2).

Today, through the inspired text of the Bible, we are equipped with the complete (Jude 3) written record of everything God has provided for our teaching, reproof, correction, and training in righteousness (2 Tim. 3:16–17). The Bible is a guidebook of scriptures for holy living, offering peace, comfort, and the true meaning and purpose of life. Being inspired by God, the Bible is our sole source of spiritual knowledge, authority, and truth.

How do we know the Bible truly is inspired by God?

- It claims to be inspired (2 Tim. 3:16). To make such a bold, confident declaration invites scrutiny, making the Bible a lightning rod for all to attack, and yet it has survived the challenge for thousands of years.
- It exhibits amazing unity. Although these sixty-six books were written in three different languages by more than forty men over a time span of 1,500 to 1,600 years, there are no conflicts or inconsistencies. There is unity and harmony in theme, content, plan, and doctrine.
- Its prophecies are accurately fulfilled both in proper timing and specific details. Examples include Jeremiah's prediction of a seventy-year captivity for Judah (Jer.

25:9–12) and Isaiah naming King Cyrus as the one who would allow rebuilding of the temple 150 years later (Isa. 44:26–28). There are some 450 Old Testament prophecies of Christ and His Kingdom.

- It reports facts impartially, telling the good and the bad about people contrary to the bias exhibited by human authors. Noah was a righteous preacher (Gen. 6) who got drunk (Gen. 9:21). David, a man after God's heart (1 Sam. 13:14), also committed adultery and murder (2 Sam. 11:1–15). The apostle Peter denied Jesus three times (Matt. 26:69–75).

- The Bible has proven to be indestructible, surviving thousands of years despite attempts to destroy it. Over 5 billion copies have been printed.

- It advocates a higher code of conduct contrary to conventional human wisdom. The Bible says to love your enemies (Matt. 5:44), to consider it joy to face trials (Jas. 1:2), and to not seek to store up treasures on earth (Matt. 6:19). These make sense based on God's higher plan only where there is life beyond the grave and the best is yet to come.

- The Bible is historically accurate in all details. Archeology has verified biblical accounts (e.g., the existence of the Hittites). New Testament facts are confirmed by Jewish historians such as Josephus. It accurately references topography, compass directions, and customs of the time.

- It is scientifically accurate, stating truths that were unknown to science until centuries later. Some examples are that the earth is round (Prov. 8:27; Isa. 40:22); the earth is suspended on nothing (Job 26:7); the universe is wearing out, which is the second law of thermodynamics (Isa. 51:6; Ps. 102:25–26); and life is in the blood (Lev. 17:11).

Pillar 3: The Problem of Sin

While the word "sin" correctly is associated with violating God's laws and commands, a more precise definition comes from the meaning of the Hebrew and Greek words found in the original inspired Bible manuscripts. These words convey the idea of "missing the mark" like an archer whose arrow strays from hitting the bull's-eye on the target. Since the intent for human beings (i.e., God's offspring) is to be holy just like our Heavenly Father, the figurative target we are to aim for is the holiness of God. When we fail to be holy by doing something unholy, we sin.

Because God is just, our sin must have consequences. God cannot simply ignore sin, for that would be unjust. When we "miss the mark" (e.g., break God's law), our sin separates us from God (Isa. 59:1–2). We are disfellowshipped because a holy God must be set apart from sin and all things unholy. To do otherwise would taint God, making Him unholy. That can never be. While the loss of God's fellowship may be tolerable during life on earth, it will not be when our spirit enters the spiritual realm. In physical death, the body decays to the dust of the earth, but the spirit is released returning to God who gave it (Eccl. 12:6–7).

In the spiritual realm, sin brings spiritual death (Rom. 6:23)—a total separation from God in eternity. To be denied fellowship with God in eternity means being deprived of all the blessings that God supplies: love, peace, joy, comfort, light, goodness, and more. With all godliness removed, all that remains are ungodly things such as hate, turmoil, sorrow, torment, darkness, and evil. This is the condition of Hell—an eternity separated from God. The Bible describes Hell in physical terms we can understand as a furnace of eternal fire with weeping and gnashing of teeth (Matt. 13:49–50;

25:41). We have never experienced such a place nor would we ever want to.

The problem of sin is "all have sinned and fall short of the glory of God" (Rom. 3:23). As a result, if left to our own means, we are all headed to Hell.

Pillar 4: God's Gift of Salvation

Fortunately, God loves us and does not want anyone to experience the hopelessness and anguish of Hell. But how can a holy God remain just and spare humanity from spiritual death? The solution required the sacrificial offering of the Son of God (John 3:16).

Jesus was a man of flesh and blood who possessed a spirit that was the Word, also known as the Son of God (John 1:1–3, 14). Being deity in the flesh (Phil. 2:5–8), Jesus was able to live a life without sin, maintaining full fellowship with the Heavenly Father and deserving no punishment for sin. Even though holy and innocent, Jesus willingly accepted the consequence for our sins in His death on the cross (1 Pet. 2:21–25). This was a perfect sacrifice of the just for the unjust once and for all (1 Pet. 3:18). Being justified by the offering of Christ, who took our place, we now have a way to escape the wrath of God, be reconciled to the Heavenly Father (Rom. 5:9–11), and gain a future home in Heaven with Him (1 Pet. 1:3–4).

The death, burial, and resurrection of Jesus prove that He is the Son of God (Rom. 1:4) and that a solution to the problem of sin exists through Him (1 Cor. 15:1–4). The question now becomes: how do we claim God's gift of salvation made available through the sacrifice of Jesus for our sins?

Pillar 5: Claiming God's Gift of Salvation

Because God gave us free will, we are able to make decisions for ourselves. It is the poor choices we have made in the past that created the sin problem in the first place. Even though God has provided a solution to the problem of sin through the death of Jesus on the cross, He still allows us the freedom to accept or reject Jesus. God does not force salvation on anyone, but rejecting Jesus is a certain path to Hell. Our sins are forgiven only through His sacrifice, offering redemption leading to an eternity with God in the glorious Kingdom of Heaven.

During His earthly ministry, Jesus taught how to be saved, mentioning four essential things that must be done (i.e., our obedience of faith) to obtain God's forgiveness. First, one must believe in Jesus as the Son of God (John 8:24). To deny this fact is to say Jesus was just another man, making Him out to be a liar and a sinner, no longer a perfect sacrifice for sin.

Second, one must repent (Luke 13:3, 5), turn away from a life of sin, and walk in the light (1 John 1:5–7) by agreeing to pursue a life of holiness. Anything less would be asking for unconditional forgiveness and freedom to continue in sin without consequence. That defies the nature of a just and holy God.

Third is confessing the belief that Jesus is the Son of God (Matt. 10:32, Rom 10:10). This confession affirms the reason for our repentance by attributing a changed lifestyle to the belief in Jesus.

The final step in the path to salvation is baptism. Jesus said, "He who has believed and has been baptized shall be saved" (Mark 16:16). The importance of baptism is confirmed by the teachings of the apostles on the Day of Pentecost, when baptism was cited as necessary to obtain the forgiveness of sins and gift of the Holy Spirit (Acts 2:38).

Based on the definition of the Greek word used in the original inspired manuscripts, we know that Christian baptism is an immersion in water. The salvation afforded in baptism does not reside in the water's physical cleansing of dirt from the flesh but rather arises from an appeal to God for forgiveness empowered through the resurrection of Jesus (1 Pet. 3:21). According to scripture, this is the way we actually call on the name of the Lord for salvation (Rom. 10:13). In the act of baptism, we are buried with Christ into His death, putting our sinful nature to death and rising a new creature (Rom. 6:3–8).

No longer separated from God by sin, each of us becomes a Christian, reconciled to God through Jesus, having the hope of eternity with God in Heaven: "But now having been freed from sin and enslaved to God, you derive your benefit, resulting in sanctification, and the outcome, eternal life" (Rom. 6:22).

CHAPTER

The First Christians

Before His ascension into Heaven, Jesus gathered the apostles for some final instructions.

> Then He opened their minds to understand the Scriptures, and He said to them, "Thus it is written, that the Christ would suffer and rise again from the dead the third day, and that repentance for forgiveness of sins would be proclaimed in His name to all the nations, beginning from Jerusalem. You are witnesses of these things. And behold, I am sending forth the promise of My Father upon you; but you are to stay in the city until you are clothed with power from on high." (Luke 24:45–49)

The promise of the Father was to provide a Helper, the Spirit of Truth (John 14:16–17)—the Holy Spirit who would guide them into all truth (John 16:13), teach, and bring to remembrance the things Jesus said (John 14:26). This was to take place in Jerusalem, where the apostles would receive power from on high (Acts 1:4–5).

Acts 2 records the miraculous events surrounding the fulfillment of God's promise. In a dramatic fashion, the apostles were filled with the Holy Spirit and began preaching to the crowds who had assembled from many nations for the Day of Pentecost, and everyone was amazed to hear the words in their own language. In his message, Peter boldly declared the deity of Jesus, His cruel death on the cross, and His resurrection from the dead according to God's plan (Acts 2:22–24).

Peter closed his remarks with words that pierced the hearts of the Jewish people: "Therefore let all the house of Israel know for certain that God has made Him both Lord and Christ—this Jesus whom you crucified" (Acts 2:36). Therein was the realization that they had witnessed and encouraged the Crucifixion of the promised Messiah, the Christ (Isa. 9:6–7). Crushed by the burden of guilt and seeking redemption from God, they cried out, pleading: "What shall we do?" (Acts 2:37). Without hesitation, Peter replied with specific instructions on what steps they must take to be redeemed.

> Peter said to them, "Repent, and each of you be baptized in the name of Jesus Christ for the forgiveness of your sins; and you will receive the gift of the Holy Spirit. For the promise is for you and your children and for all who are far off, as many as the Lord our God will call to Himself." And with many other words he solemnly testified and kept on exhorting them, saying, "Be saved from this perverse generation!" So then, those who

had received his word were baptized; and that day there were added about three thousand souls. (Acts 2:38–41)

There are several very important points to be made from these scriptures. This is the first preaching of the gospel—the good news of the death, burial, and resurrection of Jesus according to God's foreknowledge and plan to save humankind. It provides not only an example of the essential teaching but also the proper response necessary to obtain the forgiveness of sins. When people heard the truth, believed it, felt genuine remorse, and repented, they were baptized (immersed in water) in the name of Jesus for the forgiveness of their sins. This clearly depicts the process of evangelism in an account taken directly from the Bible.

Acts 2:41 says people were "added" after receiving his word and being baptized. What were they added to, and who added them? Acts 2:47 provides the answer: "And the Lord was adding to their number day by day those who were being saved" (NASB). The King James translation reads "And the Lord added to the church daily such as should be saved." Obedient believers received the forgiveness of sins and became Christians, as the Lord Himself added them to the Body of Christ, His Church.

There are many scriptures that support these facts.

- Jesus is the author of our salvation, and He determines who shall be saved (Acts 2:47).

> It is a trustworthy statement, deserving full acceptance, that Christ Jesus came into the world to save sinners, among whom I am foremost of all. (1 Tim. 1:15)

- Salvation is obtained when we obey Jesus (Heb. 5:9), submitting to God in obedience to the truth.

> For He was foreknown before the foundation of the world, but has appeared in these last times for the sake of you who through Him are believers in God, who raised Him from the dead and gave Him glory, so that your faith and hope are in God. Since you have in obedience to the truth purified your souls for a sincere love of the brethren, fervently love one another from the heart, for you have been born again not of seed which is perishable but imperishable, that is, through the living and enduring word of God. (1 Pet. 1:20–23)

- Those who have had sins forgiven are sanctified (1 Cor. 1:2) and become members of the Church.

> Husbands, love your wives, just as Christ also loved the church and gave Himself up for her, so that He might sanctify her, having cleansed her by the washing of water with the word, that He might present to Himself the church in all her glory, having no spot or wrinkle or any such thing; but that she would be holy and blameless. So husbands ought also to love their own wives as their own bodies. He who loves his own wife loves himself;

for no one ever hated his own flesh, but nourishes and cherishes it, just as Christ also does the church, because we are members of His body. (Eph. 5:25–30)

- The Body of Christ is the Church, and Jesus is its head.

    And He put all things in subjection under His feet, and gave Him as head over all things to the church, which is His body, the fullness of Him who fills all in all. (Eph. 1:22–23)

- Those who belong to the Church are called Christians.

    And he left for Tarsus to look for Saul; and when he had found him, he brought him to Antioch. And for an entire year they met with the church and taught considerable numbers; and the disciples were first called Christians in Antioch. (Acts 11:25–26)

The book of Acts, sometimes called the Acts of the Apostles, documents the founding of the Church and the spread of Christianity. For that reason, it is an excellent primer for evangelism. The gospel was preached, and when people believed, repented, and confessed Jesus as the Son of God by being baptized in His name, their sins were forgiven, and Jesus added them to His Church.

CHAPTER

Now I'm a Christian, What Next?

On the Day of Pentecost, the Jewish people were offered God's gift of salvation through the death, burial, and resurrection of Jesus. Believers who obeyed Peter's directives by repenting and being baptized in the name of Jesus were born again spiritually and restored to fellowship with God. Lives were forever changed, as the Bible says: "They were continually devoting themselves to the apostles' teaching and to fellowship, to the breaking of bread and to prayer" (Acts 2:42). This verse highlights three important aspects of their reformed lives:

1.   spiritual growth
2.   fellowship and unity
3.   worship

Spiritual Growth

Having been forgiven of their sins, these new Christians were eager to learn how to maintain that status and continue living a holy life. They were babes in Christ who needed to be taught what it means to be disciples of Jesus. That led them to turn to the very men who had preached the gospel. They sought out and acknowledged the apostles as God's messengers of truth.

Today, Christians connect with the Word of God through the writings of the apostles and the other inspired authors of the New Testament. Paul affirmed this in his letters to the Thessalonians:

> For this reason we also constantly thank God that when you received the word of God which you heard from us, you accepted it not as the word of men, but for what it really is, the word of God, which also performs its work in you who believe. (1 Thess. 2:13)

> So then, brethren, stand firm and hold to the traditions which you were taught, whether by word of mouth or by letter from us. (2 Thess. 2:15)

Through the inspired scriptures of the Bible, God has revealed everything we need to know about how to live a righteous and holy life—the life God always intended for us.

> All Scripture is inspired by God and profitable for teaching, for reproof, for correction, for training in righteousness; so that the man of God may be adequate, equipped for every good work. (2 Tim. 3:16–17)

As Christians, we are expected to study and learn the truths that God has revealed, just as Paul commanded Timothy: "Be diligent to present yourself approved to God as a workman who does not need to be ashamed, accurately handling the word of truth" (2 Tim. 2:15).

There is a parallel between our physical and spiritual developments. At birth, we require nourishment and care to grow strong physically. This transitions us from infancy through childhood into an adult status. So it is spiritually. Christians are to follow a similar trajectory, starting as immature babes who grow to spiritual maturity by feeding on the Word of God and allowing it to shape their lives (Eph. 4:11–14). Therein lies the goal: "but speaking the truth in love, we are to grow up in all aspects into Him who is the head, even Christ" (Eph. 4:15).

Fellowship and Unity

Those who responded to the call of the gospel and committed to living a holy life entered into fellowship with God (1 Cor. 1:9) and with fellow believers through the Body of Christ (1 John 1:7).

The birth of the Lord's Church created a wave of energy and excitement that brought people together. This unity in mind and spirit was an integral part of the apostle Paul's teaching. "Make my joy complete by being of the same mind, maintaining the same love, united in spirit, intent on one purpose" (Phil. 2:2).

People celebrated their common faith, offering praise to God and enjoying the company of other Christians. The prevailing attitude and camaraderie were witnessed and well received by the community at large, and the Body of Christ began to grow.

> Day by day continuing with one mind in the
> temple, and breaking bread from house to house,
> they were taking their meals together with
> gladness and sincerity of heart, praising God and
> having favor with all the people. And the Lord was
> adding to their number day by day those who were
> being saved. (Acts 2:46–47)

Christians enjoy a special relationship with God—one that makes them part of a spiritual family. Jesus referred to obedient believers as brothers and sisters (Matt. 12:50), and Paul called them members of the Household of God.

> For both He who sanctifies and those who are
> sanctified are all from one Father; for which reason
> He is not ashamed to call them brethren. (Heb. 2:11)

> But in case I am delayed, I write so that you will know
> how one ought to conduct himself in the household
> of God, which is the church of the living God, the
> pillar and support of the truth. (1 Tim. 3:15)

The spiritual bond that ties Christians together transcends physical differences in status, race, culture, and gender.

> For you are all sons of God through faith in Christ
> Jesus. For all of you who were baptized into Christ
> have clothed yourselves with Christ. There is
> neither Jew nor Greek, There is neither slave nor
> free man, There is neither male nor female; for you
> are all one in Christ Jesus. (Gal. 3:26–28)

Christians are children of God (1 John 3:1) and are taught to have a deep and abiding love for one another (1 John 4:7), not acting selfishly but looking out for the interests of others (Phil. 2:3–4).

Worship

The converts of Acts 2 were eager to express their gratitude and devotion to God, and they did so in worship. Explicitly mentioned among the spiritual offerings found in Acts 2:42 are the breaking of bread and prayer. In context, the breaking of bread references what is commonly known as "communion" or "the Lord's Supper"—clearly not referring to a typical family meal because it appears in a list of spiritual offerings. The social aspect of families gathering to eat meals together actually is discussed later in verse 46.

It is important to realize that the Jewish people had to learn a new pattern of worship adopted under the Christian age. This was no doubt part of the apostles' teaching. The Old Covenant was replaced by the New Covenant (Heb. 8:6–7), and the worship practices of the Old Covenant were set aside. For example, there was no longer a need for animal sacrifices. Jesus was offered as a sacrifice for sins once for all, the just for the unjust (1 Pet. 3:18).

> But He, having offered one sacrifice for sins for all time, sat down at the right hand of God, waiting from that time onward until His enemies be made a footstool for His feet. For by one offering He has perfected for all time those who are sanctified. (Heb. 10:12–14)

Through His death on the cross, Jesus became our mediator, providing the link necessary to reconnect humankind to the God (1 Tim. 2:5–6). Hence, there is no longer a need or role for an intermediary priest. Christians are a royal priesthood having gained access to God through Jesus (1 Pet. 2:9–10).

Christian worship is directed only to Deity. When people attempted to worship the apostle Peter or even angels, they were rebuked.

> When Peter entered, Cornelius met him, and fell at his feet and worshiped him. But Peter raised him up, saying, "Stand up; I too am just a man." (Acts 10:25–26)

> I, John, am the one who heard and saw these things. And when I heard and saw, I fell down to worship at the feet of the angel who showed me these things. But he said to me, "Do not do that. I am a fellow servant of yours and of your brethren the prophets and of those who heed the words of this book. Worship God." (Rev. 22:8–9)

Worship is an expression of love and gratitude, giving thanks, praising, honoring, and treating God as holy. Jesus said, "God is spirit, and those who worship Him must worship in spirit and truth" (John 4:24). Our offerings to God must come from the heart, worshipping not as we choose but rather as God has directed. It is an act of submission and devotion that we do to adore and please Him, not ourselves.

Through the recorded history of the New Testament Church, we can learn how Christians worshipped God. There are both examples and directives issued by the apostles. Therein can be found five elements of Christian worship.

1. The Lord's Supper

On the first day of the week, Christians assembled to partake of the Lord's Supper (Acts 20:7). This consisted of unleavened bread and fruit of the vine, representing the body and blood of Jesus who was sacrificed for our sins. The practice was instituted by Jesus during a celebration of the Jewish Passover (Matt. 26:26–30; Mark 14:22–26; Luke 22:14–20) and serves four purposes:

1. It is foremost *communion*—a sharing or participation in the body and blood of Jesus (1 Cor. 10:15–17).
2. It is a *commemoration*—a memorial in remembrance of the sacrifice Jesus made for the forgiveness of our sins (Luke 22:19; 1 Cor. 11:24–25).
3. It is a *proclamation* whereby Christians are proclaiming the death of Jesus with the conviction that He is coming again to claim His own (1 Cor. 11:26).
4. It is a time for *self-examination* when Christians are to focus on the price that was paid for their individual sins (1 Cor 11:28–32).

2. Prayer

The apostle Paul referred to prayer as an expression of his heart's desire (Rom. 10:1). Christians communicate to God in prayers offered through the name of Jesus, our mediator (John 14:13–14), and those prayers typically involve some of the following elements:

- **adoration**, acknowledging God as the supreme holy spiritual being He is—the eternal, omnipresent, omniscient, omnipotent Creator of all things (Matt. 6:9; Gen. 1:1; John 1:1–3)
- **thanksgiving**, expressing thanks and gratitude for what God has done (Col. 4:2; Phil. 4:6; Heb. 13:15)
- **intercession**, prayer on behalf of others (Jas. 5:16: John 17:9–21; 2 Thess. 1:11; 1 Thess. 5:25)
- **confession**, acknowledging our own sin (1 John 1:9; Mark 11:25)
- **supplication** or petition, asking or making requests of God (Matt. 7:7–11; 1 Tim. 2:1–3)

3. Singing

Christians offer praise and thanks to God through the fruit of the lips singing, making melody with their hearts to the Lord, and admonishing one another with psalms, hymns, and spiritual songs.

> Through Him then, let us continually offer up a sacrifice of praise to God, that is, the fruit of lips that give thanks to His name. (Heb. 13:15)

> So then do not be foolish, but understand what the will of the Lord is. And do not get drunk with wine, for that is dissipation, but be filled with the Spirit, speaking to one another in psalms and hymns and spiritual songs, singing and making melody with your heart to the Lord. (Eph. 5:17–19)

> Let the word of Christ richly dwell within you,
> with all wisdom teaching and admonishing one
> another with psalms and hymns and spiritual
> songs, singing with thankfulness in your hearts
> to God. (Col. 3:16)

From church history, we know this was a cappella singing, voice without instrumental accompaniment. Christians worship by communicating through words, not empty sounds (1 Cor 14:7–9). It is to be a meaningful expression from the heart directed to God. This is not done for human esthetics, pleasure, or satisfaction. It is done to please God according to His will.

4. Teaching and Preaching the Word of God

God's revelation provides the spiritual food that strengthens Christians by teaching us how to live a holy life and mature to a Christlike status (Col. 1:24–29; 2 Tim. 4:1–5). Since that revelation has been captured in the inspired writings of the Bible (2 Tim. 3:16–17), the Bible is our sole source of spiritual truth and authority.

5. Giving

Christians set aside money on a weekly basis to give to the work of the Church according to how they have prospered (1 Cor. 16:1–2). These financial resources are used to help the needy (Acts 4:34–35), care for widows and orphans (1 Tim. 5:3–10; Jas. 1:27), and support evangelism (1 Cor. 9:13–14; Luke 10:7; 1 Tim. 5:17–18).

A Benevolent People

Another characteristic of Christian living involves caring for others. The Christians of Acts 2 shared what they had with those in need, mindful that many had traveled to Jerusalem for Pentecost and found themselves without resources for a much longer stay.

> And all those who had believed were together and had all things in common; and they began selling their property and possessions and were sharing them with all, as anyone might have need. (Acts 2:44–45)

> And the congregation of those who believed were of one heart and soul; and not one of them claimed that anything belonging to him was his own, but all things were common property to them. And with great power the apostles were giving testimony to the resurrection of the Lord Jesus, and abundant grace was upon them all. For there was not a needy person among them, for all who were owners of land or houses would sell them and bring the proceeds of the sales and lay them at the apostles' feet, and they would be distributed to each as any had need. (Acts 4:32–35)

The apostle Paul stressed the importance of doing good to all people, especially to brothers and sisters in Christ.

> Let us not lose heart in doing good, for in due time we will reap if we do not grow weary. So

then, while we have opportunity, let us do good to all people, and especially to those who are of the household of the faith. (Gal. 6:9–10)

A Forgiven People

It is not easy to live a holy life patterned after Jesus. Christians are still human and do sin, be it from ignorance or weakness giving in to temptation. The good news is Christians have an advocate in Jesus.

But if we walk in the Light as He Himself is in the Light, we have fellowship with one another, and the blood of Jesus His Son cleanses us from all sin. If we say that we have no sin, we are deceiving ourselves and the truth is not in us. If we confess our sins, He is faithful and righteous to forgive us our sins and to cleanse us from all unrighteousness. (1 John 1:7–9)

A faithful Christian is blessed by being able to go to God in prayer, confessing faults and asking for forgiveness, in which case God promises to grant that forgiveness through the cleansing blood of Jesus. However, this is not to be taken as an excuse to sin. Paul rejected that notion.

What shall we say then? Are we to continue in sin so that grace may increase? May it never be! How shall we who died to sin still live in it? (Rom. 6:1–2)

Christians are expected to walk in the light and grow continuously by dwelling in God's word and learning from past mistakes and life experiences.

For though by this time you ought to be teachers, you have need again for someone to teach you the elementary principles of the oracles of God, and you have come to need milk and not solid food. For everyone who partakes only of milk is not accustomed to the word of righteousness, for he is an infant. But solid food is for the mature, who because of practice have their senses trained to discern good and evil. (Heb. 5:12–14)

An Evangelistic People

When persecution fell upon the early church and the Christians were being driven out of Jerusalem, "those who had been scattered went about preaching the word" (Acts 8:4). They took their beliefs with them to foreign lands, sharing the good news of Jesus. These were an evangelistic people just as God had always intended. So it should be said of all Christians.

Christianity is meant to be shared. It offers meaning and purpose to life and provides hope beyond the grave. That is why God has committed to all Christians the ministry of reconciliation (2 Cor. 5:18–19). It is why Paul called Christians "ambassadors for Christ, as though God were making an appeal through us" (2 Cor. 5:20).

CHAPTER

Transforming Lives
with the Truth

CHRISTIANS ARE GOD'S TRUTH TELLERS, DELIVERING A message that can transform lives into what they were always intended to be, bringing peace during troubled times on earth and hope for the future—eternal life with God in Heaven. However, to fully appreciate how truth is able to transform lives, we must first understand what it is.

What is truth?

Most people associate the concept of truth with facts based on physical reality. This is a "human truth" deduced from observations and life experiences accumulated over time. While this definition sounds reasonable, it restricts truth to human discovery in the physical realm and produces a set of relative principles, subject to change based on new findings and better understanding. In this limited worldview, absolute truth is unattainable because it requires absolute knowledge, and no human being can meet that standard.

The truth that transforms is Divine Truth. It does not originate in the minds of humans, nor does it come from findings in the physical world. Its source resides with God, a Spirit from another realm who purposefully designed and created the physical universe and everything in it, including life itself. Divine Truth stems from the absolute knowledge of the Creator and encompasses not only the principles governing our physical domain but also the more important truth about the existence of a spiritual realm beyond the reach of human discovery.

Being the source of all substance and life, God alone commands absolute knowledge providing the gateway to absolute truth. The scriptures declare Him to be the God of Truth (Ps. 31:5; Isa. 65:16) abounding in truth (Exod. 34:6) with a truth that is everlasting (Ps. 117:2). Likewise, Jesus asserted His claim to truth as the Son of God, saying: "I am the way, and the truth, and the life; no one comes to the Father but through Me" (John 14:6). As the Spirit Being who designed and created the universe (Exod. 20:11), God knows the truth by who He is and what He did.

Over the ages, God has communicated the truth to humankind in many portions and in many ways (Heb. 1:1–2): in words (2 Sam. 7:28; Ps. 119:160), commandments (Ps. 119:51), and law (Ps. 119:142) given through the prophets. But for us today, God has revealed Himself through His Son, and that truth has been captured in the inspired writings of the Bible.

Why is transformation important?

The best advice for those who find themselves trapped in a deep hole is to stop digging. Through selfish desires, foolish actions, or sheer ignorance, all of us have managed to fall short of God's expectations and thereby place ourselves in that proverbial deep hole. In the process, we have created personal hardships, hurt others, and more importantly managed to alienate ourselves from the Creator. These things have profound implications not only for life on earth but for what awaits us after death. A divine transformation is needed to get us back on the right track.

Human nature draws us to things we like. Good food, tasty drinks, enjoyable company, pleasurable experiences, recreation, and stimulating entertainment can provide healthy outlets from the day-to-day drudgeries of life. However, even healthy pursuits can become harmful when taken to excess. Add to that the long list of unhealthy things offering short term highs, and it is easy to see how we can fall into patterns of bad behavior that lead to personal suffering and long-term destructive outcomes. Such is the fate of many who have become impoverished by the selfish pursuit of worldly pleasures. Drug and alcohol addictions, diseases, divorce, broken friendships, crime, financial ruin, and legal troubles are just some of the possible physical outcomes. These add needless pain and suffering to what is often already a difficult existence. The truth can direct us to a better way of life.

Even more important than the physical predicaments of life are the spiritual consequences of being alienated from the Creator when we defy His will for us by leading an unholy life. Being created in the image of God (Gen. 1:26–27), humans were endowed not only with a physical body but also with an eternal spirit. In physical death, that spirit returns to the Creator who gave us life

(Eccl. 12:7). For those who have not been transformed by the truth, there awaits an eternal separation from God in the anguish and torment of Hell. God wants all humankind to hear and obey the truth and be transformed into His Kingdom, leading to eternal life in Heaven (1 Tim. 2:3–4).

How does the Truth transform?

Divine Truth transforms troubled lives by revealing the error of our ways and directing us to the lifestyle God always intended for humanity. Following His guidance not only leads to an improved quality of life on earth but also restores our broken relationship with God and holds the promise of an enduring peace beyond the grave in Heaven with Him.

Many people live their whole life by trial and error, learning what seems to work through the "school of hard knocks," unaware that there is a divine instruction manual for how to live. While life experience can be a great teacher, it also comes with a cost. The self-inflicted pain from poor choices can hurt not only the individual but also innocent bystanders, producing effects that can last for a lifetime. Wouldn't it be nice to possess guidelines guaranteed to keep us away from needless pitfalls while providing all the ingredients essential for a meaningful, productive, and happy life? The Creator of the universe has provided these guidelines in the truth revealed through the Bible.

It is rare that we are given an opportunity for a do-over. Indeed, the harm created by a careless word or thoughtless deed often has a snowball effect that follows us our entire life. That does not mean we cannot try to make things right as best we can, nor does it keep us from resolving to do better in the future. These choices are ours to make, but we must live with the consequences of our actions. That is how things work in the physical realm.

Amazingly, we are blessed with the opportunity for a completely fresh start when it comes to our spiritual relationship with the Creator. No matter what the circumstances may be, sinners—those who have missed the mark set by God's holiness—always can obtain forgiveness and be reconciled to God through Jesus as revealed by the truth. This offers hope for everyone willing to submit to God's will. Not only does this concession lead to a better life on earth, it also secures a future home in Heaven with God when we die. By revealing the existence of the spiritual realm, truth inspires us to set our sights on something higher—a future beyond this earthly existence.

God's truth transforms lives by purifying our hearts and changing the way we think about things. As our attitude changes, so too does our behavior. Those who put aside selfish desires and pattern their lives after the nature of a holy God can live the fulfilling, productive life God always wanted for humankind and enjoy the promise and prospects of eternal life with Him. The truth transforms by offering:

> **The enlightenment of telling us who we really are.** Our prospects and personal identity encompass who we are, where we came from, and where we are going. This is valuable information influencing how we live our life on earth. Having created humankind in His own image (Gen. 1:26–27) and having designed the world for our dwelling, God is uniquely positioned to teach us how to be good stewards, meeting His expectations and preserving fellowship with Him.

Knowing the truth about our spiritual identity and the existence of life beyond the grave is essential for us to be able to make informed decisions and properly prepare for the future.

The meaning and purpose of life. The significance of life lies in our role as a created being with responsibilities to the Creator. We are not our own. God expects us to honor and serve Him by living a holy life patterned after His nature. In return, as faithful children of God, we are promised an eternal reward in the spiritual realm when our physical existence comes to an end. This gives us the true meaning and purpose of life.

Knowledge of our spirit and the spiritual realm. Although we can infer the existence of a Creator from the intelligent design, vastness, and working complexity of the universe, we are unable to explore other spiritual realities beyond our physical realm. That revelation of truth must come from God. It is He who commands the knowledge to share intimate details about our dual nature—possessing not only a physical body but an eternal spirit crafted in the image and likeness of God. The existence of the spiritual realm and life beyond the grave would be totally unknown to us were it not for the truth revealed by God. This knowledge changes our whole perspective about life and death on earth and gives us the motivation to trust and honor God.

Awareness of the threat of Hell. When we sin by rebelling against God, living the selfish life we choose instead of the holy life He expects, our fellowship with God is severed. Iniquities separate us from Him (Isa. 59:1–2) and put us at risk of spending eternity in the anguish of Hell. It is important for us to understand the severe consequences of an eternity separated from God and thereby separated from all the blessings He provides. This is valuable information needed to make informed decisions about how to prepare for what comes after physical death.

A path to reconciliation. While it is true that "all have sinned and fall short of the glory of God" (Rom. 3:23), it is also true that God loves us and wants to preserve our fellowship with Him. However, that is not an easy task. A just and righteous God cannot indiscriminately forgive disobedience and sin. Justice must be preserved. To redeem humankind, He who was without sin, namely Jesus, the Son of God, willingly sacrificed Himself, taking the burden for sins in His death on the cross. This was God's plan to save humankind by giving us the option to claim the sacrifice of Jesus as payment for our sins.

Salvation through Jesus Christ. Although God offers forgiveness and salvation as a free gift through Jesus, we must still acknowledge and accept that gift. God does not force Himself on anyone. The truth tells us how to claim His gift by our obedience of faith (Rom. 16:25–26; Heb. 5:9) when we answer the call of the gospel (2 Thess. 2:14) by believing, repenting, confessing Jesus as the Son of God, and being baptized into Christ.

Guidance for a fulfilling life on earth. By learning how to live a holy life in a corrupt world, we model behavior that can influence others for good. This influence promotes the development of friendships and has a lasting impact on those around us. Furthermore, it leaves a good legacy and brings the personal satisfaction of knowing we have made a difference in this world.

Wisdom. Truth is the source of all wisdom: "For the LORD gives wisdom; From His mouth come knowledge and understanding" (Prov. 2:6). Just as it is important to learn how we should live, it also is important to learn what things we should avoid. A misplaced love of the world and the things in the world (1 John 2:15) can bring us to ruin. Materialism draws us away from the more important spiritual realities. Being physical in nature, it is easy for us to be tempted by the lust of the flesh, the lust of the eyes, and the pride of life (1 John 2:16). "Trust in the LORD with all your heart and do not lean on your own understanding. In all your ways acknowledge Him, And He will make your paths straight" (Prov. 3:5–6).

A code of conduct defining moral and ethical behavior. What are the basic principles of moral and ethical behavior, and how do we go about defining them? The truth that transforms instructs us to pattern our lives after God. We are to be Holy as He is Holy (1 Pet. 1:14–16). The truth is we must avoid immorality, impurity, sensuality, idolatry, sorcery, enmities, strife, jealousy, outbursts of anger, disputes, dissensions, factions, envying, drunkenness, carousing, and other things like these (Gal. 5:19–21) and instead embrace love, joy, peace, patience, kindness, goodness, faithfulness, gentleness, and self-control (Gal. 5:22–23). Moreover, we find a perfect example through the life of Jesus revealed in the New Testament books of Matthew, Mark, Luke, and John.

Integrity, values, and a set of priorities for living. Armed with the truth, we need no longer be "tossed here and there by waves and carried about by every wind of doctrine, by the trickery of men, by craftiness in deceitful scheming" (Eph. 4:14). We possess a standard of living defined through the truth of the Bible. This truth not only provides guidance in matters of personal conduct but gives us tangible incentives for living a holy life. God is a rewarder of those who seek Him (Heb. 11:6). By knowing the truth, we are able to properly prioritize the choice between physical and spiritual things.

A cure for loneliness. Those who submit to God's will become Christians—true disciples of Jesus. That instantly makes them part of the Lord's Church, enjoying fellowship with a large community of other believers all over the world. These are people who love God and have a genuine love and concern for one another.

A spiritual family and support network. Individuals who have embraced the truth of God are blessed by being a part of the Body of Christ (the Church), a family of believers made up of many spiritual brothers and sisters who stand ready to help in all aspects of life. All of us struggle with day-to-day challenges, whether they be physical or spiritual. No longer must we endure mourning the loss of a loved one, illness, financial need, depression, or temptations while all alone. There is a loving community able and willing to offer help and encouragement in times of need.

Clearly, God's Divine Truth has much to offer and can transform lives, offering blessings beyond measure. But if lives are to be changed, then the truth must be heard. Delivering that teaching is the responsibility that has been placed in the hands of each and every Christian.

CHAPTER

Some Closing Thoughts

As the Crucifixion drew near, Jesus comforted His apostles with words to carry them through the difficult days ahead.

> A new commandment I give to you, that you love one another, even as I have loved you, that you also love one another. By this all men will know that you are My disciples, if you have love for one another. (John 13:34–35)

The key thought was loving one another. This was true for His disciples then, and it is true today, especially for those who are losing someone dear to their heart. The best thing we can do is to love them. Jesus said that loving one another was to be a distinguishing characteristic—a trait that the world would use to identify His followers.

Although we recognize the need to comfort and love people

when a dear friend or family member passes away, we tend to overlook the greater tragedy of lost souls who, though physically alive, are spiritually dead and face an eternity in Hell. Ironically enough, this is the one case where our love is capable of bringing the dead back to life. We can do it by teaching them how to answer the call of the gospel to attain eternal life ... and yet, do we do it?

This book was written to equip and encourage Christians to share the gospel—the good news of Jesus Christ. However, we have an adversary (1 Pet. 5:8). The devil stands in the way, wanting us to sit on the sidelines and do nothing. There is no shortage of excuses he can bring to mind to create roadblocks preventing us from getting involved. Some of these obstacles are summarized in Table 2 along with strategies to overcome them that are discussed in this book and in the articles, audio, videos, slides, study outlines, and teaching template available on the website at TheTruthTransforms.com.

Table 2. Obstacles that often prevent Christians from continuing Christ's mission of seeking and saving the lost, and some strategies for overcoming these obstacles.

Obstacle	Strategies for Overcoming
Why me?	You have been chosen, for "He has committed to us the word of reconciliation. Therefore, we are ambassadors for Christ, as though God were making an appeal through us" (2 Cor. 5:19–20).
I can't do it.	Yes, you can: "I can do all things through Him who strengthens Me" (Phil. 4:13).
I don't know how to get started.	See "How to Initiate Bible Studies," chapter 14; audio and article at the website.
I don't know how to teach.	See "Recommendations for Bible Study Leaders," chapter 16; audio and article at the website.

I don't know what to teach.	See "A Teaching Template," chapter 17; downloadable file at the website; and "The Good News of Jesus Christ," chapter 18; audio and article at the website.
I am willing to host a Bible study, but I need someone else to do the teaching.	Multimedia presentations of "The Good News of Jesus Christ" and "The Five Pillars of Truth" are available as videos, audio, and slides at the website.
I know people who need to hear the gospel, but they don't want to meet for a Bible study.	Distribute the link to the website at www.TheTruthTransforms.com
I want to do more but don't know what to do.	See "Often Missed Opportunities," chapter 15. Other things to do: Share the link to the website at www. TheTruthTransforms.com. When sharing the website link with others, ask them to do likewise by passing it on. Build a team of workers who distribute the website links through emails, texts, and posting on social media and websites. Promote and give away books on God's plan of salvation and evangelism, including *A Debt I Cannot Pay* and *Continuing Christ's Mission*

The Lord's Admonition

In the Old Testament, the Lord appointed the prophet Ezekiel as a watchman for the house of Israel. His mission was to deliver a warning to the people when he received a message from the Lord. Particularly noteworthy is the fact that God held the watchman accountable for fulfilling that mission, and if he failed to warn the people, his own life was at risk.

> Now as for you, son of man, I have appointed you a watchman for the house of Israel; so you will hear a message from My mouth and give them warning from Me. When I say to the wicked, 'O wicked man, you will surely die,' and you do not speak to warn the wicked from his way, that wicked man shall die in his iniquity, but his blood I will require from your hand. But if you on your part warn a wicked man to turn from his way and he does not turn from his way, he will die in his iniquity, but you have delivered your life. (Ezek. 33:7–9)

As ambassadors for Christ (2 Cor. 5:20), Christians bear a responsibility to continue Christ's mission by sharing the message of Jesus with the lost. We do this to teach people the truth and warn them about the threat of Hell so they can make an informed decision about their eternal future. It is a sobering thought to realize that Christians are the watchmen of the New Testament.

What will *you* do with Jesus? This is a question that is aptly posed to Christians and non-Christians alike, and the answer is equally important to both groups. To the lost, it is a decision about whether to answer the call of the gospel and receive salvation with the gift of eternal life or to reject Jesus and be separated from God for eternity in Hell. To the Christian, it is a decision about whether to fulfill the duties of a watchman by sharing the message of Jesus with others or to forsake the commission that God has given to warn the lost about the dangerous threat to their souls. May God help us all to make the right decision.

Printed in the United States
by Baker & Taylor Publisher Services